Secret Services

The Hidden Machinery of Power

Milenko Srećković

Contents

Introduction

Secret services occupy a peculiar place in the modern imagination. They are often imagined as hidden puppeteers behind world events or as glamorous networks of brilliant spies moving effortlessly through conspiracies and lies. Both images are appealing, and both are misleading. Real intelligence agencies are bureaucratic institutions shaped by law, politics, technology, secrecy, and human limitation.

Secret services are essential instruments of state power in contemporary politics, wars, and crises. Although they are often presented as neutral tools of collective security, in many historical contexts they have also enabled governing elites to control, filter, and interpret information in ways that serve particular political and strategic interests. Modern governments decide whether to go to war, sign a treaty, launch a strike, or suppress dissent on the basis of what intelligence agencies selectively reveal, conceal, or interpret. In many documented cases, such decisions have protected existing economic interests, geopolitical advantage, and established social hierarchies as much as, or even more than, genuine public safety.

Yet the public picture of intelligence work is dominated less by archival evidence and serious research than by films, novels, thriller narratives, and conspiracy theories. Popular culture has given us suave agents, infallible gadgets, and secret cabals that manage global events from luxurious underground rooms. Conspiracy culture offers a darker but equally simplistic mirror image: an idea that nothing significant ever happens without a hidden plan by some faceless "service." In both versions, intelligence agencies appear as shadowy magicians standing outside normal politics, almost detached from law, institutions, and error.

This book draws a line between those myths and the real institutions that operate under the name of secret services. Its purpose is explanatory rather than sensational: it does not promise revelations or thriller-style plots, but examines how secret services work, how they fit into the machinery of the modern state, and how secrecy, uncertainty, political power, and public freedom intersect. Because much of intelligence work is hidden, gaps in knowledge are easily filled with imagination, fear, and propaganda. For that reason, the book distinguishes documented fact from plausible interpretation and both from conjecture. Where documents, testimonies, public reports, parliamentary inquiries, court judgments, investigative journalism, and serious research exist, the book uses them; where sources are fragmentary, it marks the limits of what can responsibly be said.

The analysis that follows is grounded in intelligence studies and related fields, including history, political science, international relations, security studies, law, sociology, psychology, critical security studies, and research on surveillance capitalism and digital control. It synthesizes those lines of research into a coherent, accessible narrative. It builds on established findings where there is broad agreement, and it presents the main arguments where scholars disagree. Comparative examples from different countries and regimes are used to show how structures and practices vary with constitutional orders, political cultures, threat environments, and social conflicts.

The chapters that follow move from definition and history to failure, law, oversight, authoritarian abuse, and digital transformation. They examine why intelligence services fail, how they can drift toward political policing, and how democratic systems try to restrain secret power through parliaments, courts, watchdogs, journalists, and civil society. The book gives priority to well-documented case studies using them to clarify broader structures rather than to create a catalogue of every intelligence service and every operation.

Throughout, several interconnected questions remain at the center of the analysis: Whose security do secret services actually protect: the security of citizens and communities, or the stability of existing political and economic arrangements? Can institutions historically embedded in unequal political and economic systems be constrained to serve genuine collective safety rather than reproduce existing inequalities? And does the rule of law provide meaningful limits on intelligence power, or can it also legitimize the protection of established property relations and hierarchical social orders while narrowing the space for resistance?

In the digital sphere, power relations between individuals, states, and large corporations have changed in qualitative ways, not just grown in quantitative terms. The combination of mass data collection, commercial profiling, and state access to private databases creates a three-way asymmetry: citizens are simultaneously the object of state surveillance, a source of profit for private actors, and raw material for intelligence assessments. This asymmetry does not merely generate new security tools; it erodes some of the core assumptions of democracy by building infrastructures of continuous visibility that can be repurposed for control. In such an environment, the key question is no longer only whether surveillance is formal or covert, but who participates in building and operating these systems, and whether a political order that monitors by default can still plausibly claim to treat citizens as free and presumptively innocent.

The book's normative starting point is left-critical: intelligence services should be examined not only as administrative or security institutions, but also as instruments that can reinforce state power, class hierarchy, and unequal social relations. Their legitimacy therefore cannot rest solely on procedural oversight; it must also be evaluated in relation to inequality, dissent, and the broader public good. At the same time, the book pragmatically examines existing mechanisms for constraining intelligence power within liberal-democratic and other political systems, recognizing that even imperfect limitations can reduce harm while more fundamental transformations remain distant.

Above all, the book treats secret services as one of the places where uncertainty, state power, secrecy, and public freedom meet. Understanding them is therefore part of understanding how power works in the contemporary world.

What Secret Services Really Are

When a terrorist attack succeeds, when a coup unfolds overnight, when a war begins without warning, or when a scandal exposes years of hidden surveillance, the same question returns almost instinctively: where were the secret services? Behind that question lies a powerful assumption–that somewhere inside the state there must be a single hidden machine that sees more than everyone else, understands more than it admits, and can intervene before events escape control.

But real intelligence work is rarely so clean. There is no single dark room from which history is managed. There are agencies, departments, analysts, informants, intercepts, databases, rivalries, legal limits, political pressures, and human mistakes. Sometimes they reveal what others cannot see; sometimes they miss what later appears obvious.

To understand secret services, we must first replace the image of one mysterious actor with a more precise question: what kind of institution is collecting knowledge, who controls it, what may it legally do, and whose interests does it serve?

At the most basic level, secret services are specialized state bodies tasked with collecting, processing, analyzing, and providing information relevant to what states define as "security." Yet that definition is never politically neutral: it often reflects priorities such as state survival, regime stability, economic order, and public safety, while giving different weight to different social groups. They do help governments make informed decisions, but they also serve broader functions: maintaining political order, managing dissent, protecting strategic interests, and navigating geopolitical competition through forms of surveillance and control. What counts as a "threat"–terrorism, espionage, subversion–is itself shaped by political priorities and by the question of whose security is being protected.

Intelligence, Security, and Counterintelligence

The first conceptual distinction is between intelligence and security services, and between both of these and counterintelligence and political police.

Foreign intelligence services focus primarily on external actors and environments. Their mission is to collect information about other states, international organizations, armed groups, transnational networks, and strategic developments beyond the national territory. They try to answer questions such as: What are rival governments planning? How are their armed forces configured? Which alliances are forming or breaking? What technological advances might change the balance of power? Their work is outward-looking, even if the methods they use–human sources, interception of communications, imagery, and open-source analysis–sometimes cross legal and geographical boundaries in complex ways.

Domestic security services, by contrast, look inward. They are usually tasked with protecting the constitutional order, public safety, and critical infrastructure from threats that arise within or directly affect the state itself. These threats include terrorism, violent extremism, espionage, sabotage, organized crime, and activities intended to overthrow or seriously destabilize the political system through unlawful means. Ideally, domestic security services concentrate on serious threats rather than on peaceful political opposition or normal social conflict. When they drift into monitoring lawful dissent, journalism, or civil activism, they begin to cross the line into something closer to political police.

Counterintelligence, in turn, is concerned with detecting, understanding, and neutralizing the work of other intelligence services. It is the intelligence service's mirror image and opponent. Counterintelligence services try to discover foreign spies, prevent the theft of secrets, protect sensitive institutions and technologies, and ensure that their own agencies are not penetrated or manipulated. This work involves security vetting, surveillance, deception, double-agent operations, and defensive protection of personnel, systems, and facilities. Counterintelligence can be embedded inside foreign or domestic agencies, or it can be organized as a separate service.

In practice, these categories often overlap. A single agency may combine domestic security and counterintelligence tasks. Another may perform both foreign intelligence and covert action. Still others may be responsible mainly for technical collection on behalf of the entire intelligence community. "Secret services" should therefore be understood as a cluster of functions: gathering information about the outside world, protecting the state from internal and external threats, and protecting the intelligence system itself from hostile penetration.

The Thin Line Between Intelligence and Political Policing

A crucial distinction is often drawn between intelligence services in liberal democracies and institutions that act as political police. The distinction matters, but it is not always as clear as official language suggests.

In democratic systems, intelligence and security services are formally presented as institutions that protect the state, the constitutional order, and the public. Their legal mandates usually speak the language of national security, public safety, and lawful protection against threats such as terrorism, espionage, sabotage, and violent extremism. In principle, they are not supposed to serve a party, a ruler, or a particular ideological project.

Political police, by contrast, operate more openly as instruments of regime survival. They monitor, intimidate, and neutralize domestic opponents in order to protect a specific leadership, party, or ideological order. They keep files on citizens for explicitly political reasons, fabricate or exaggerate threats, and use security language to justify repression. In such systems, secrecy functions less as protection against external enemies and more as a shield against public accountability.

The difference between the two is therefore real, but it is also fragile. An agency formally called an intelligence service can move toward political policing when it routinely targets lawful dissent, disrupts social movements, monitors journalists, or treats opposition as a security problem rather than a legitimate part of public life. Conversely, agencies with authoritarian roots can sometimes be brought partly under legal and democratic constraint, although such reforms rarely erase their institutional habits overnight.

The key issue is not only what an agency is called, but how it defines threats, who controls it, what limits bind it, and whose interests its work ultimately serves. Legal oversight, public accountability, and constitutional safeguards can reduce abuse and create space for resistance. But they do not automatically remove the deeper tension at the heart of intelligence power: the same tools that can protect society from real dangers can also be used to preserve existing political and economic arrangements.

When secrecy operates within rule-of-law frameworks, subject to parliamentary oversight and judicial review, intelligence can be constrained from the worst excesses of political repression. When secrecy is tied to fear, party loyalty, and unchecked executive power, the same tools become machinery of domination. The most difficult question about a secret service is therefore not only how much it knows, but whom its knowledge serves.

Intelligence, Corporate Interests, and Social Movements

While the distinction between intelligence services and political police matters in practice, both forms have sometimes been drawn into the protection of existing property relations, corporate interests, and political order. This dimension is often less visible than espionage or counterterrorism, but it is important for understanding how definitions of "security" can expand beyond immediate physical threats.

Surveillance of Labor Organizing

Intelligence and security services in capitalist democracies have at times treated labor militancy as a security concern. In the United States, the FBI monitored labor organizers and infiltrated unions during parts of the twentieth century, especially under anti-communist frameworks. British security services have also been accused, and in some cases documented, of monitoring trade unionists and industrial militancy, especially during periods of intense conflict such as the miners' strikes.

Such cases show how labor conflict can be reframed as a matter of public order or economic stability. When workers challenge working conditions, wage relations, or corporate power, intelligence attention may shift from preventing violence to monitoring movements that disturb established economic arrangements. In these moments, the boundary between protecting national security and protecting corporate interests becomes blurred.

Protection of Corporate Interests Through Economic Intelligence

Intelligence services have also been used to support economic and industrial priorities. Officially, this is often presented as protecting national competitiveness, strategic industries, or technological advantage. In practice, however, the benefits may flow unevenly, including to particular firms or sectors.

Examples include allegations of Western economic intelligence being used to assist national corporations, French economic espionage in support of domestic companies, close links between Israeli intelligence units and the technology sector, and the Chinese model in which state security and economic strategy are explicitly intertwined. These examples raise a basic question: when intelligence serves the "national interest," which groups within the nation actually benefit?

Targeting Social Movements and Anti-Capitalist Organizing

Social movements have also been treated as security concerns, especially when they challenge dominant economic or political arrangements. Environmental groups, anti-globalization activists, racial justice organizers, anti-war movements, and anti-capitalist networks have all faced surveillance in different liberal democracies.

In some cases, such monitoring has been justified by concerns about extremism, disorder, or public safety. Yet many targets were not primarily violent actors; they were movements contesting inequality, corporate power, war, policing, or environmental destruction. This shows how the language of security can translate social conflict into a problem of state protection and public order.

Taken together, these patterns suggest that intelligence power does not operate only at the boundary between state and foreign enemy. It can also operate inside society, where struggles over work, property, inequality, and political dissent are sometimes recoded as questions of security.

Intelligence or Political Police? The Stasi in the GDR

The Ministry for State Security of the German Democratic Republic – better known as the Stasi – formally presented itself as an intelligence and security service tasked with protecting the socialist state from external enemies and internal subversion. In practice, it evolved into one of the most intrusive systems of political policing in modern history. Rather than focusing on concrete threats such as terrorism or espionage in a narrow sense, the Stasi devoted enormous resources to monitoring, intimidating, and neutralizing political dissent, independent culture, churches, and even informal circles of friends.

By the 1980s, the Stasi maintained files and index-card systems concerning millions of people, relying not only on professional officers but on a vast network of unofficial collaborators embedded in workplaces, neighborhoods, and social organizations. Surveillance included opening mail, tapping phones, planting bugs in homes, and systematically collecting personal information that could be used for subtle "corrosion" (Zersetzung)[1] of opponents' lives – sabotaging careers, friendships, and family relations without visible arrests or show trials. The line between "security" and control over everyday life effectively disappeared.

On paper, the Stasi claimed to protect the state and society; in reality, its primary mission was to protect the ruling party and its ideological project. Targets were selected not by the seriousness of any violent threat, but by political unreliability, criticism, or mere non-conformity.

The Intelligence Community

In most modern states, intelligence work is divided among several agencies that together form an intelligence community. This community may include:

A foreign intelligence service responsible for external collection and analysis.

A domestic security or internal intelligence service focused on internal threats.

A military intelligence service embedded in the armed forces.

Specialized technical agencies that handle signals intelligence, cyber operations, or satellite imagery.

Analytical bodies that synthesize information from multiple sources into strategic assessments for senior decision makers.

These agencies vary widely in culture, structure, and political weight. Some are dominated by military traditions; others are civilian, legalistic, or strongly bureaucratic. Some focus heavily on covert human operations; others have grown around technical capabilities and data systems. Together, they form a fragmented but interconnected web of institutions that must cooperate to provide a coherent picture to political leaders.

Fragmentation has both advantages and disadvantages. On the positive side, multiple agencies can provide diversity of perspective and specialization. Redundant channels of analysis can reduce the risk that a single institutional bias will distort the entire picture. On the negative side, fragmentation can produce rivalry, duplication, and dangerous gaps in information sharing. Agencies can withhold

---

1. Zersetzung, literally "decomposition" or "disintegration", was a Stasi method of psychological and social destabilization used against perceived opponents in East Germany. Rather than relying only on arrest, it aimed to damage reputations, careers, friendships, families, and mental stability through covert interference and manipulation.

information from one another for reasons of prestige, turf protection, or distrust, with serious consequences for warning and crisis response.

How an intelligence community is organized is therefore never a purely technical question. It reflects deeper choices about centralization versus pluralism, secrecy versus accountability, and efficiency versus checks and balances. Highly centralized systems can be fast and powerful but also prone to abuse and groupthink. Looser systems can be more cautious and diverse but may struggle with coordination. There is no perfect model; there are only different trade-offs shaped by history and politics.

One State, Many Services: The U.S. Intelligence Community

The United States is a clear example of how modern states rarely rely on a single, monolithic "secret service," but on a whole community of agencies with different mandates and cultures. Foreign intelligence is primarily the domain of the Central Intelligence Agency (CIA), which focuses on collecting and analyzing information about other states, non-state actors, and global developments outside U.S. territory. Domestic security and counterterrorism within the United States fall mainly to the Federal Bureau of Investigation (FBI), which combines law-enforcement powers with internal intelligence functions.

Alongside these, the Defense Intelligence Agency (DIA) concentrates on military-related intelligence for the armed forces, while the National Security Agency (NSA) serves as the country's main technical and signals intelligence organization, operating large-scale interception and code-breaking capabilities. Above and between them stands the Office of the Director of National Intelligence (ODNI)[2] , created after 9/11 to coordinate the wider "intelligence community" and to provide integrated assessments for senior decision makers.

This fragmentation brings advantages and risks. Specialisation allows agencies to develop expertise in human intelligence, domestic counterterrorism, military analysis, signals intelligence, or cyber operations. Overlapping perspectives can also reveal blind spots. Yet dispersed responsibility creates coordination problems:

---

2. The Office of the Director of National Intelligence (ODNI) was created after 9/11 to coordinate the U.S. intelligence community and provide integrated intelligence assessments to senior policymakers. Its creation reflected the belief that fragmented agencies had failed to share and synthesize information effectively before the attacks.

agencies may compete for influence, protect information, or interpret legal limits differently. In crisis, the system works only if these separate bureaucracies cooperate in practice.

People, Not Only "Spies"

Popular images of secret services emphasize spies: individuals living under false identities, infiltrating organizations, stealing documents, or recruiting agents. Human sources and clandestine officers do remain important. But the internal reality of intelligence agencies is less romantic and more bureaucratic than such images suggest.

Secret services are staffed by analysts, translators, linguists, data scientists, engineers, lawyers, auditors, liaison officers, administrators, and technical specialists as well as field officers and agents. Analysts interpret information; they are the ones tasked with connecting dots, challenging assumptions, and presenting judgments to decision makers. Technical staff maintain interception systems, databases, and networks. Legal advisers and internal auditors interpret mandates, review operations, and try to ensure compliance with law and policy. Liaison officers manage relationships with foreign services, sharing some information while protecting sensitive sources and methods.

This bureaucratic and professional dimension matters because it reminds us that secret services are organizations, not mystical entities. They have recruitment policies, promotion patterns, internal cultures, and informal norms. They suffer from bureaucratic inertia, communication problems, and institutional blind spots just like other large organizations. Their successes and failures are as much a product of these internal dynamics as of their access to secrets.

Intelligence as Information, Process, and Institution

The word "intelligence" itself is ambiguous. It has at least three distinct meanings, and confusion arises when they are not clearly separated.

First, intelligence refers to information, particularly information that has been collected, processed, and evaluated to support decisions. In this sense, a report on a terrorist network, a satellite image of a missile site, or an assessment of a foreign government's intentions are all "intelligence."

Second, intelligence refers to a process–the set of activities through which information is turned into actionable knowledge. This includes setting priorities, collecting data, verifying sources, analyzing patterns, debating interpretations, and presenting conclusions along with their uncertainties. When people speak of "the intelligence cycle," they are referring to this process.

Third, intelligence refers to institutions: the organizations, both individual agencies and the wider community, that conduct these activities. When someone says "intelligence believed that..." they often mean that the relevant agencies, as institutions, collectively held a certain view.

The ambiguity becomes dangerous when the three senses are blurred. If "intelligence" is treated as some abstract, unified entity that simply "knows," it becomes easy to overestimate what agencies can do, to underestimate their internal disagreements, and to ignore the ways in which information can be distorted as it moves through the process from source to decision. Separating information, process, and institution helps to restore realism.

Institutional Power

Secret services clearly possess significant power. They can access information that ordinary citizens and even many officials never see. They can influence political decisions by shaping what leaders believe about threats and opportunities. In some systems, they also run covert operations that can affect events directly–supporting allies, undermining opponents, or manipulating narratives.

That influence depends on the environment in which it operates: legal mandates, oversight, resources, technology, adversary behavior, internal culture, and the willingness of leaders to hear unwelcome assessments.

Seen more precisely, there is no single, unified "secret service," but a set of distinct yet interconnected agencies operating under different mandates, staffed by fallible people, and embedded in the political systems they serve.

How Intelligence Works

A WARNING RARELY ARRIVES as a clear sentence. More often, it appears as a fragment: an unusual movement of vehicles near a border, a sudden silence in a communications channel, a source who says that "something is being prepared," a satellite image that shows more activity than expected, a message intercepted but not fully understood. None of these fragments, taken alone, may be enough to prove anything. Together, they may point toward a crisis. Or they may point toward nothing at all.

This is the daily problem of intelligence work: how to turn incomplete, uncertain, and sometimes contradictory pieces of information into a judgment that someone in power can use. The stakes can be enormous. A misunderstood signal can produce panic. A missed signal can leave a country unprepared. A warning delivered too late may become useless. A warning delivered too confidently may push leaders toward unnecessary escalation.

Behind every intelligence assessment lies a chain of choices: what was asked, collected, ignored, interpreted, communicated, and finally heard. Intelligence is the difficult movement from question to evidence, from evidence to judgment, and from judgment to action.

The Intelligence Cycle from Tasking to Decision

Intelligence work is often imagined as a collection of isolated secret missions: a source recruited here, a phone tapped there, a document stolen in some distant capital. In reality, secret services operate through a structured process that connects political questions at the top with raw information at the bottom and then back again to decision-makers. This process is commonly described as the intelligence cycle. The cycle is not a rigid machine–real life is messier–but it is a useful way to understand how data becomes assessment, and assessment becomes part of political choice.

From Questions to Tasks: Direction and Planning

Every intelligence effort begins not with collection but with questions. Political leaders, senior officials, and security managers need to know certain things: whether a rival state is preparing for war, whether a terrorist group is plotting attacks, whether a new weapon is being developed, whether a cyber operation is underway against critical infrastructure. These needs are expressed as intelligence requirements.

The first phase of the cycle–often called direction or planning–is about translating those broad concerns into specific tasks for the intelligence community. What exactly must be found out? Which gaps in knowledge are most dangerous? What deadlines and priorities are involved? Which agencies and capabilities are best suited to the problem? Intelligence leaders turn these questions into collection plans that specify what kind of information is needed and where it might be obtained.

This phase is crucial because intelligence services do not and cannot collect everything. The world produces more data than any system can absorb. Choices about what to look for and what to ignore shape everything that follows. Poorly framed requirements, vague priorities, or purely political demands for confirmation of what leaders already believe will distort the entire process before a single piece of information is gathered.

Gathering the Raw Material: Collection

Once priorities and plans are set, agencies move to the collection phase. Here, they use a range of methods–some open, some secret–to obtain raw information relevant to the defined requirements. The main collection disciplines are often summarized with a set of acronyms.

Human intelligence (HUMINT)[1] is information gathered from people. It includes clandestine sources who secretly provide access to internal deliberations, plans, or capabilities; overt interviews; debriefings of defectors or returnees; and contact with officials, businesspeople, or others who have insight into important developments. HUMINT can provide unique access to intention–a sense of what leaders are planning or fearing–but it is also vulnerable to deception, manipulation, and personal bias.

Signals intelligence (SIGINT) refers to information derived from communications and other electronic emissions. This can include intercepted phone calls, emails, data traffic, radio communications, radar signals, and other electronic flows. SIGINT can reveal patterns of activity and sometimes concrete plans, but it depends heavily on technological access and can be disrupted by encryption, secure channels, or changes in adversary behavior.

Imagery intelligence (IMINT) uses visual collection platforms–from aircraft and satellites to drones and other sensors–to capture images of facilities, equipment, troop movements, and terrain. It is particularly valuable for monitoring physical changes over time, such as construction at missile sites or mobilization of forces. Its limitations include weather, concealment, and the need for careful interpretation.

Open-source intelligence (OSINT) uses publicly available information: media reports, academic studies, government documents, commercial satellite imagery, social media, trade data, and more. In the digital era, OSINT has become a major component of intelligence work, but it presents its own challenges of verification and information overload.

Measurement and signature intelligence (MASINT) and related technical disciplines focus on distinctive scientific or technical signatures, such as specific radar profiles, chemical traces, or unique patterns associated with certain systems. These methods can detect activities that are otherwise hidden, but they require advanced sensors, specialized expertise, and careful integration with other streams of information.

---

1. HUMINT refers to intelligence gathered from human sources; SIGINT to intercepted communications and electronic signals; IMINT to imagery from aircraft, satellites, drones, or other visual platforms; OSINT to publicly available information; and MASINT to technical signatures such as radar, chemical, nuclear, or acoustic traces. These categories often overlap in practice, and modern intelligence assessments usually combine several of them.

Real-world collection rarely relies on a single discipline. Effective intelligence uses a mix of methods, cross-checking one stream against another to reduce the risk of deception and misinterpretation. But whatever the method, what is collected at this stage is still only raw material–fragments, not yet knowledge.

Making Data Usable: Processing

The collection phase can produce enormous volumes of raw data: intercepted communications, sensor feeds, imagery, documents, reports from human sources. Before analysts can make sense of this material, it must be processed.

Processing includes sorting, indexing, decrypting, translating, and formatting information so that it can be retrieved and understood. It may involve converting signals into readable form, tagging documents with metadata, organizing imagery into searchable databases, and placing human-source reports into standard formats that clarify who said what, on what basis, and with what degree of confidence.

This stage is sometimes underestimated in public discussion, but it is a major source of both strength and vulnerability. Well-designed processing systems help ensure that relevant information can be found and used when needed. Poorly designed systems can bury important signals under a mountain of noise, mislabel data in ways that hide its significance, or introduce delays that make otherwise good information arrive too late.

From Fragments to Judgments: Analysis and Production

Analysis sits at the heart of the intelligence process. Analysts take processed information from multiple sources and try to turn it into coherent assessments for decision-makers. They must answer questions such as: What is happening? Who is involved? What does it mean? What might happen next? What are the main alternative explanations, and how confident can we be?

Good analysis is more than a summary of incoming reports. It requires evaluating the reliability of sources, understanding the context in which information was produced, identifying patterns across different disciplines, and being explicit about assumptions and gaps. Analysts must constantly ask themselves how they could be wrong, what evidence would contradict their current view, and whether they are ignoring uncomfortable possibilities.

The tools of analysis can range from simple chronologies and maps to complex models, network diagrams, and data-driven methods. But the core remains human judgment informed by experience, training, and critical thinking. Analysts must communicate not only what they think is most likely, but also how strong the evidence is, what alternatives exist, and what the implications are for policy choices.

The products of analysis vary in form and frequency. They can include daily briefs for senior leaders, warning notes about emerging threats, in-depth reports on specific issues, and long-term strategic assessments. In crises, the tempo of production accelerates, but the underlying tension remains: the need to provide timely advice without pretending that uncertainty has disappeared.

Delivering Intelligence: Dissemination and Use

Even the best analysis is useless if it does not reach the right people at the right time in a form they can absorb. The dissemination phase is about delivering intelligence products to the decision-makers for whom they are intended.

This can involve secure digital systems, face-to-face briefings, written reports, or oral presentations. The format depends on the urgency, sensitivity, and complexity of the issue. Highly technical assessments may require explanatory sessions; short warnings may need to be delivered directly and quickly. In all cases, intelligence must compete for attention in crowded political schedules.

The value of intelligence is measured not only by its accuracy but by its effect on decisions. Leaders may act on a warning, adjust a policy, reconsider a negotiation, or delay a risky move because of what intelligence reveals. But leaders may also ignore or downplay intelligence that does not fit their preferences, ideology, or political interests. The relationship between intelligence and decision-making is thus never automatic. It is shaped by trust, credibility, and the broader political environment.

Completing the Loop: Feedback and Adaptation

The final step of the intelligence cycle is often described as evaluation or feedback. After intelligence has been used–or not used–agencies and consumers should assess what worked and what did not. Were the questions well framed? Was relevant information collected? Were the processing systems adequate? Did analysis capture key developments and uncertainties? Did the products arrive in time and in a useful form?

In principle, this feedback should inform new priorities, adjust collection plans, refine analytic methods, and improve communication between services and decision-makers. In practice, feedback is uneven. Busy political leaders may not take the time to review how they used intelligence. Agencies may resist criticism or find it difficult to admit structural weaknesses. Political sensitivities may discourage honest examination of failures. Where feedback is weak, the same patterns of error are likely to repeat.

Intelligence as a Continuous, Imperfect Process

The intelligence cycle is sometimes criticized for being too neat, as if intelligence work were a clean sequence of discrete steps. In reality, stages overlap. New information can change priorities, prompting rapid re-tasking. Analysts may guide collection by asking for specific types of information. Decision-makers may request deeper analysis on short notice. Emergencies can compress the cycle into frantic, iterative loops.

Despite its simplifications, the cycle remains a valuable model. It shows that intelligence depends as much on planning, processing, analysis, and communication as on any particular secret source. Its value lies not only in gathering secrets, but in asking the right questions and presenting decision-makers with judgments that make uncertainty clearer rather than more comforting.

Intelligence is therefore best understood as a discipline, not a possession. Secrets, sources, satellites, intercepts, and databases matter only if fragments are turned into honest judgment before events overtake decision-makers. At every stage, rigor and institutional humility can strengthen intelligence; haste, ambition, bureaucracy, and political pressure can weaken it.

The Intelligence Cycle in Practice: The Cuban Missile Crisis[2], 1962

The discovery of Soviet nuclear missiles in Cuba in October 1962 is a classic example of how the intelligence cycle works from initial tasking to political deci-

2. The Cuban Missile Crisis was a thirteen-day confrontation in October 1962 between the United States and the Soviet Union after U.S. reconnaissance revealed Soviet nuclear missile sites in Cuba. It is widely treated as one of the most dangerous moments of the Cold War, when intelligence, diplomacy, military planning, and political restraint were all tested under the risk of nuclear escalation.

sion. In the months before the crisis, President John F. Kennedy and his advisers had already tasked U.S. intelligence with monitoring Soviet activities in Cuba, worried that the island might be used for a significant military build-up. This political concern was translated into concrete collection priorities: increased aerial reconnaissance, closer monitoring of shipping, and heightened attention to any signs of new missile deployments in the Western Hemisphere.

Collection began to pay off when U-2 reconnaissance flights over Cuba produced high-resolution photographs of suspicious installations. Imagery analysts identified launch pads, missile erectors, and support equipment consistent with Soviet medium-range ballistic missiles, while other sources – including signals intelligence on Soviet and Cuban communications – helped confirm that this was not merely defensive equipment or conventional artillery. The raw imagery and intercepts then had to be processed: films developed, frames indexed and annotated, intercepted signals decrypted, translated, and sorted. Only once this material had been stabilized and organized could it be integrated into a coherent picture.

The analysis phase was crucial. Analysts compared the Cuban sites with known Soviet missile deployments elsewhere, assessed ranges and capabilities, and estimated how quickly the missiles could become operational. They evaluated alternative explanations (for example, whether the sites might be for different weapons systems) and judged that the evidence strongly supported the conclusion that the Soviet Union was secretly deploying nuclear-armed missiles within striking distance of major U.S. cities. These assessments, with their associated confidence levels and timelines, were turned into concise intelligence products for the top leadership.

Dissemination took the form of briefings to the president and his inner circle. Kennedy was shown key photographs and received written and oral assessments summarizing what was known, what was uncertain, and what the likely Soviet intentions might be. Intelligence did not dictate a particular policy, but it framed the menu of options – from doing nothing, through diplomatic protest, to an air strike or naval quarantine. As the crisis unfolded, feedback and adaptation completed the cycle: new reconnaissance flights were tasked to monitor Soviet reactions and the pace of construction; updated analysis refined estimates of readiness and risk; and the results were fed back into the ExComm's deliberations.

Throughout the thirteen days of the crisis, intelligence and policy remained in continuous dialogue. Political decisions – such as choosing a naval quarantine rather than an immediate air strike – in turn reshaped intelligence priorities, focusing collection on Soviet ships approaching the quarantine line and on any signs that the missiles in Cuba were being readied for launch. The Cuban Missile

Crisis thus illustrates the intelligence cycle not as a neat, one-off sequence, but as a rapidly iterating process in which tasking, collection, analysis, dissemination, and feedback constantly informed one another under intense time pressure, with potentially catastrophic consequences if either intelligence or decision-making failed.

Operational Blindness: When OSINT[3] Outruns Traditional Services

In the months before Russia's full-scale invasion of Ukraine in February 2022, open-source analysts, journalists, and hobbyists used commercial satellite imagery and social-media posts to track the Russian build-up near Ukraine. Images from private providers and videos from TikTok, Instagram, and other platforms helped observers map units, estimate force levels, and identify likely axes of advance before official announcements.

For governments, this created an unusual tension. Classified systems were also tracking Russian movements, but official material had to pass through slower processing and analytic pipelines. OSINT analysts, by contrast, could combine commercial imagery, social-media videos, and geolocation techniques into near-real-time public maps. The episode showed that the bottleneck for secret services is no longer only access to information, but the ability to process, fuse, and communicate it at the speed of open sources.

3. OSINT, or open-source intelligence, became especially visible before Russia's full-scale invasion of Ukraine in February 2022, when journalists, researchers, and independent analysts used commercial satellite imagery, social media videos, transport data, and geolocation techniques to track Russian military deployments. The case showed that some intelligence-like functions can now be performed publicly, outside traditional state agencies.

A Short History of Secret Services

Long before intelligence agencies had headquarters, archives, analysts, listening stations, satellites, or encrypted databases, rulers faced the same old fear: what are my enemies planning, who inside my court is loyal, and where will the next danger come from? A king waiting for news from a distant frontier, an emperor suspicious of a provincial governor, a general uncertain about the strength of the army across the river–all depended on information that was incomplete, delayed, and often deliberately hidden.

In that world, intelligence did not yet look like a modern institution. It moved through messengers, merchants, scouts, diplomats, informers, prisoners, priests, servants, and travelers. A rumor overheard in a market, a sealed letter carried across a border, a report from a frontier commander, or a whisper inside a palace could alter decisions of war, succession, alliance, or repression. The methods were primitive, but the political instinct was already modern: power belongs not only to those who command armies, but also to those who know what others are preparing.

The history of secret services is not simply the history of spies. It is the history of how states learned to organize suspicion, preserve secrecy, collect knowledge, and turn information into a permanent instrument of rule.

From Ancient Espionage to the Cold War Intelligence State

Secret services did not appear suddenly in the twentieth century as fully formed bureaucracies. The institutions described in earlier chapters are the product of a long evolution in which rulers gradually learned to treat information as a strategic resource, then built permanent organizations to supply it. To understand why modern intelligence agencies became such a central part of state power, it is necessary to trace that evolution–from early espionage in empires and courts, through the professionalization of the nineteenth century, to the globalized intelligence states of the world wars and the Cold War.

Early Espionage: Empires, Courts, Trade, and War

Wherever there were rulers who feared enemies, rivals, and rebellion, there were also attempts to gather secret information. Ancient empires deployed scouts, messengers, and informants to monitor distant territories, tributaries, and potential foes. Imperial courts used trusted servants and envoys to report on intrigues, alliances, and plots. The methods were rudimentary by modern standards, but the logic was familiar: a ruler who knew what others planned enjoyed an advantage over a ruler who did not.

Espionage in early societies took several overlapping forms. Military commanders relied on scouts and spies to learn about enemy troop movements, fortifications, and supply lines. Merchants and travelers carried news about political changes, market conditions, and new routes, often sharing or selling their knowledge to authorities. Court officials watched for signs of disloyalty among nobles and administrators. In some systems, rulers cultivated networks of informers or "eyes and ears" to hear what subjects said in taverns, markets, and temples.

These practices were episodic and personal rather than institutional and bureaucratic. They depended on individual initiative and ad hoc arrangements, not on permanent agencies with defined mandates and procedures. The quality and continuity of information varied with the personality of the ruler and the stability of the regime. When a strong leader valued intelligence, networks were maintained and expanded; when a successor lost interest, they decayed. Secret communication–through codes, ciphers, and sealed letters–was known, but still limited in scope.

Despite these limitations, early espionage showed a pattern that would repeat throughout history: information was sought most intensely where rulers felt most vulnerable. Threats at the frontier, rival courts, restive provinces, and contested trade routes all generated demand for secret knowledge. The difference in later centuries would not be the discovery of espionage itself, but the creation of permanent institutions to manage it.

Professionalization and Bureaucratization in the Nineteenth and Early Twentieth Centuries

The nineteenth century transformed the landscape of intelligence. Industrialization, mass armies, expanding empires, and modern bureaucracy all pushed states toward more systematic ways of gathering and using information. As warfare became more complex and railways, telegraphs, and mass conscription changed the speed and scale of mobilization, governments could no longer rely solely on ad hoc spies and occasional reports.

In many European powers, the first permanent intelligence structures grew out of military needs. General staffs began to establish dedicated sections responsible for studying foreign armies, collecting information on potential adversaries, and preparing war plans. These sections compiled order-of-battle data, maps, rail timetables, and assessments of terrain and logistics. They also began to experiment with more organized forms of intelligence collection, including peacetime networks in key cities and border regions.

At the same time, the expansion of colonial empires created new demands for information about distant societies, political movements, and local elites. Colonial administrations developed their own intelligence systems, mixing political reporting with police surveillance and anthropological observation. Metropoles tried to integrate these flows of information into their strategic thinking, though the results were uneven and often shaped by prejudice and misunderstanding.

Political authorities also started to build more systematic internal surveillance structures. As urbanization, industrialization, and mass politics grew, governments worried about labor unrest, revolutionary movements, and nationalist agitation. Police forces created specialized branches to monitor political groups, gather information on agitators, and infiltrate organizations deemed subversive. In some monarchies and empires, these branches evolved into powerful political police with extensive networks of informers.

What distinguished this period from earlier eras was the gradual emergence of bureaucracy. Intelligence and security functions were assigned to specific offices, budgets, and career tracks. Personnel were recruited, trained, and promoted within hierarchical organizations. Procedures were formalized, archives established, and reporting channels standardized. Intelligence began to look less like a sporadic accompaniment to statecraft and more like a routine, institutionalized function of the modern state.

This transformation turned intelligence from an occasional instrument of rulers into a permanent function of the modern state. Files, offices, procedures, trained personnel, and institutional memory gave governments new power, but also created new dangers. Once suspicion becomes a bureaucracy, it can protect society from real threats, but it can also acquire momentum of its own.

Precursors of Modern Services: The Tsarist Okhrana

The Okhrana[1], the secret police of late imperial Russia, stood at the intersection of political policing and intelligence work. Formally tasked with protecting the tsarist regime from revolutionaries and foreign threats, it developed an extensive network of informers and undercover agents who infiltrated socialist, anarchist, and nationalist groups at home and abroad. Its officers monitored émigré circles in European capitals, collected information on foreign governments, and tracked revolutionary fundraising and propaganda networks, blurring the line between external intelligence and domestic repression.

Inside the empire, the Okhrana operated as a classic political police force. It kept surveillance files on suspected opponents, intercepted mail, infiltrated opposition organizations, and used both open repression and subtle manipulation to weaken underground movements. In some cases, Okhrana agents not only penetrated revolutionary groups but helped organise and steer them, creating ethically and politically ambiguous situations in which state agents facilitated the very conspiracies they were supposed to prevent.

The history of the Okhrana links early forms of political policing to later totalitarian practices. Many basic techniques that would be perfected in the twentieth century – systematic informant networks, extensive dossiers, covert infiltration, and the fusion of domestic surveillance with broader security and foreign-policy concerns – were already present in late tsarist Russia. At the same time, the Okhrana's ultimate failure to save the regime illustrates a recurring theme: even highly intrusive secret police structures cannot indefinitely stabilise a political order that is losing its social and political legitimacy.

1. The Okhrana was the secret police of late imperial Russia, especially active from the late nineteenth century until the 1917 Revolution. It monitored revolutionary, socialist, anarchist, nationalist, and émigré groups through surveillance, informers, infiltration, and political repression, making it an important precursor to later modern political police systems.

World War I and the Expansion of Organized Intelligence

The First World War accelerated these trends. It was a conflict of unprecedented scale, fought by mass armies using industrial weapons across multiple fronts. To sustain such a war, states needed reliable knowledge of enemy capabilities, plans, and vulnerabilities. Intelligence was no longer a luxury; it became a necessity.

During the war, military and naval intelligence structures expanded dramatically. Signals interception and cryptanalysis grew in importance as armies and fleets relied heavily on telegraph and radio communications. Codebreaking units were established to exploit intercepted messages, revealing operational plans and strategic intentions when successful. Aerial reconnaissance and photography supplemented traditional scouting, providing new ways to observe enemy positions and movements.

Internal security services intensified their efforts to counter espionage, sabotage, and dissent. Governments monitored foreign nationals, censored mail and telegrams, and cracked down on perceived disloyalty. Political intelligence and propaganda intertwined as states sought both to protect themselves from enemy agents and to maintain morale at home. The boundaries between intelligence, police work, censorship, and political control became blurred.

The war also showed the limits of intelligence. Despite organizational growth, there were still major failures of anticipation and understanding. Prewar assumptions distorted interpretation of data; inter-service rivalries hindered sharing; and decision-makers sometimes ignored unwelcome assessments. Nonetheless, by the end of the conflict, intelligence and security structures were far more developed and entrenched than they had been before 1914.

World War II: Codebreaking, Deception, and Strategic Intelligence

If the First World War strengthened the roots of modern intelligence systems, the Second World War made them central trunks of state power. The conflict mobilized societies and technologies on an even greater scale, and intelligence played a crucial role in multiple theaters.

One of the most striking developments was the rise of large-scale codebreaking and signals intelligence. States invested heavily in intercepting enemy communications and in building teams and machines to break complex ciphers. Successful codebreaking provided insights into enemy operations, logistical constraints, and strategic thinking that could not be obtained by other means. It enabled more effective use of limited resources, better timing of operations, and sometimes the avoidance of catastrophic surprises.

Deception operations also reached new levels of sophistication. Intelligence services and military planners combined false information, controlled leaks, dummy equipment, and double agents to mislead adversaries about the timing and location of major operations. Strategic deception required a deep understanding of how the enemy interpreted signals, what they considered credible, and how to manage multiple channels of information over time.

Strategic intelligence, in the sense of sustained analysis of enemy capabilities, intentions, and vulnerabilities at the highest level, became a recognized function. Intelligence assessments informed decisions about where to allocate industrial production, how to prioritize theaters of war, and which alliances to cultivate. They also played a role in evaluating the development of new weapons, including rockets and nuclear programs.

Internal security services, meanwhile, were tasked with countering foreign espionage, protecting key technologies, and ensuring loyalty in a time of existential threat. Their methods ranged from surveillance and arrests to cooperation with resistance movements and partisans in occupied territories. Again, the lines between security, repression, and political control were not always clear, especially in authoritarian regimes.

By the end of the Second World War, many states had created a dense infrastructure of intelligence, security, and codebreaking organizations. They had invested in training, technology, communication systems, and coordination mechanisms that would not simply disappear when peace returned. Instead, they provided the foundation for the next phase: the intelligence state of the Cold War.

Ultra and Enigma[2]: When SIGINT Changes the Course of War

During the Second World War, Britain's breaking of German Enigma codes and the wider Ultra programme showed how institutionalised signals intelligence

---

2. Enigma was a German cipher machine used to encrypt military communications during the Second World War. "Ultra" was the codename for intelligence derived from Allied codebreaking, especially at Bletchley Park, where intercepted German communications were decrypted, analyzed, and distributed to selected commanders and political leaders.

(SIGINT) and analysis can shape both battles and high-level strategy. Enigma-encrypted radio traffic carried orders, situation reports, and logistical details for the German armed forces. By capturing these signals and systematically attacking the ciphers at Bletchley Park, British codebreakers turned what was meant to be unbreakable communication into a powerful window on German intentions and capabilities.

The value of Ultra did not lie only in brilliant cryptanalysis, but in the entire institutional system that grew around it. Intercept stations had to collect vast volumes of traffic; specialized teams decrypted and translated messages; analysts sifted, cross-checked, and fused them into coherent assessments; and a carefully controlled distribution system delivered the most sensitive insights to selected commanders and political leaders. When it worked well, this SIGINT allowed the Allies to reroute convoys away from U-boat wolfpacks, anticipate Luftwaffe raids, and understand the shifting deployment of German forces on multiple fronts.

At the operational level, Ultra contributed to concrete outcomes: for example, by revealing U-boat patrol lines in the Battle of the Atlantic, it helped reduce shipping losses to a level that made sustained transatlantic supply possible; by disclosing aspects of German dispositions before key campaigns, it informed British and Allied planning in North Africa and Europe. Strategically, it gave decision-makers a more accurate picture of German strengths and weaknesses than would have been possible through human intelligence and reconnaissance alone.

At the same time, the Ultra story also illustrates the limits and dilemmas of powerful SIGINT. To protect the secret that Enigma had been broken, commanders could not always act on every piece of decrypted information, and sometimes had to accept avoidable losses to avoid revealing the source. Intelligence still had to be interpreted within a broader context, weighed against other information, and translated into politically and militarily feasible options. Even at its most successful, SIGINT did not "win the war on its own," but it decisively tilted the balance by making Allied decisions better informed and more timely than they would otherwise have been.

The Cold War Intelligence State: CIA, KGB, MI5/MI6, Stasi, and Others

The Cold War transformed intelligence from a wartime necessity into a permanent feature of international politics. The prolonged confrontation between nuclear-armed blocs, the risk of global war, and the ideological struggle between competing systems made information and secrecy central to strategy.

In this environment, foreign intelligence services such as the CIA and the Soviet KGB (along with its successor organizations) became key instruments of national power. They were tasked not only with collecting information about each other's military capabilities and political intentions, but also with conducting covert operations around the world. These operations included support for allied governments and movements, attempts to influence elections, coups, propaganda, and various forms of political warfare short of overt conflict.

Domestic security services like MI5 in the United Kingdom and internal departments within the KGB were responsible for counterintelligence and internal security. They monitored suspected spies, tracked ideological opponents, and sought to prevent infiltration and subversion. In liberal democracies, this often produced tension between security concerns and civil liberties; in communist and authoritarian systems, internal security services frequently acted as political police, suppressing dissent and enforcing conformity.

The British MI6 and other external services of allied states played important roles in gathering information on the Soviet bloc, the decolonizing world, and emerging conflicts. Intelligence alliances grew in importance, with states sharing data, analysis, and technical capabilities within blocs. Joint listening posts, shared codebreaking projects, and multinational assessment bodies reflected the reality that intelligence, like security more broadly, had become deeply embedded in alliance structures.

Perhaps nowhere was the fusion of intelligence and repression more visible than in the East German Stasi. It developed an extensive network of informers and surveillance mechanisms that penetrated almost every aspect of society. Files were kept on vast numbers of citizens; conversations were monitored; and careers, relationships, and personal lives were affected by the pervasive presence of the secret police. While extreme, this example illustrates how, in some regimes, intelligence and security structures became not just tools of foreign policy but core instruments of domestic control.

Across both blocs, the intelligence apparatus became a permanent, institutionalized part of the state. Budgets, personnel, and legal frameworks expanded. Secret services developed internal cultures, career paths, and professional identities. Technological advances, especially in signals interception and imagery, spawned specialized agencies. Intelligence and security considerations influenced foreign policy, defense planning, and internal governance in ways that made them integral to the functioning of modern power.

Stasi as an Infrastructure of Surveillance

The Ministry for State Security (Stasi) of the German Democratic Republic did not emerge fully formed as an all-seeing apparatus. Created in 1950, it grew out of the Soviet security model and quickly evolved from a relatively small state security office into a sprawling bureaucracy at the heart of the East German "intelligence state." Its formal mission was to protect the socialist state from espionage, sabotage, and "enemy-negative elements," but in practice this came to mean continuous scrutiny of almost every sphere of social life. Over the decades, the Stasi expanded its headquarters in Berlin-Lichtenberg into a dense administrative complex and built a network of regional and local offices that penetrated towns, factories, universities, and even small villages.

Surveillance was not improvised; it was organized as an infrastructure. The Stasi relied on tens of thousands of full-time officers and a vast number of unofficial collaborators (Inoffizielle Mitarbeiter) who reported on colleagues, neighbours, and even family members. It systematically intercepted mail, tapped telephones, monitored border crossings, and collected physical samples (such as scent traces) to assist future tracking by dogs. Technical departments developed and maintained an array of eavesdropping devices, photography equipment, and document-handling systems. Over time, the service accumulated millions of files, card indexes, and dossier fragments that could be combined to reconstruct a citizen's associations, attitudes, and vulnerabilities.

These techniques were embedded in a broader strategy known as Zersetzung – "decomposition" – which aimed not only to arrest or openly punish opponents, but to subtly destabilise their lives. The Stasi used its knowledge to block career opportunities, sow mistrust in social circles, strain marriages, and create a constant sense of being watched. In this way, surveillance became less a series of discrete operations and more a permanent, infrastructural condition shaping everyday behavior.

Historically, the Stasi illustrates what an "intelligence state" within the socialist bloc could look like: an institutionalised fusion of domestic intelligence, political policing, and social control, supported by extensive bureaucratic and technical resources rather than by ad-hoc terror alone. It shows how a secret service can become a central organiser of social order in an authoritarian system, and why dealing with its archives and legacies after regime change poses such profound challenges for transitional justice and democratic reconstruction.

Similar patterns of fusion between intelligence and political policing appeared in Latin American military regimes and in parts of the Middle East, where services formally tasked with national security became central instruments of regime protection.

Intelligence as Political Police: Brazil, Turkey, and Egypt

In many discussions, the archetype of political police is drawn from European experiences: tsarist Russia's Okhrana or the East German Stasi. Yet similar fusions of intelligence, internal security, and regime protection have appeared across Latin America and the Middle East, often under very different historical and social conditions. Brazil's military dictatorship, Turkey's National Intelligence Organization (MİT), and Egypt's Mukhabarat illustrate three variations of the same pattern: services formally tasked with defending the state that became central instruments of domestic control, repression, and the management of political opposition.

In Brazil, the military coup of 1964 opened two decades of authoritarian rule in which intelligence and security organs formed a layered system of surveillance and repression. Ministries, military commands, and police forces maintained overlapping intelligence units that targeted left-wing militants, unionists, students, and perceived subversives. The National Truth Commission later documented killings, disappearances, systematic torture, violations against Indigenous communities, and the penetration of universities, media, and civil society. The Brazilian case shows how political policing can become a multi-level bureaucracy whose legacy outlives the generals who built it.

Turkey's National Intelligence Organization (MİT) became a key node in the security apparatus during the Cold War, linking alliance intelligence, domestic counter-insurgency, and internal political policing. After the 1980 military coup, intelligence and security services helped guard a re-engineered political order. Later conflicts, especially against Kurdish movements and other perceived threats, kept blurring the line between national security and regime protection.

In Egypt, mukhabarat became closely associated with secret police power. Under Nasser, Sadat, and Mubarak, intelligence and security bodies combined foreign intelligence with extensive domestic monitoring of political life. They suppressed the Muslim Brotherhood, leftist groups, independent unions, liberal activists, journalists, and human-rights organizations, while emergency laws and anti-terrorism frameworks gave repression a legal vocabulary. The result was a durable security state in which surveillance and detention helped govern society long before and after moments of open crisis.

Together, Brazil, Turkey, and Egypt show that the slide from intelligence to political policing is not uniquely European or tied to one ideology. Under Cold War and anti-terrorist narratives, services formally tasked with national security became instruments for managing domestic opposition and protecting ruling orders.

From Episodic Espionage to Infrastructural Intelligence

Across this evolution, early espionage gave way to professionalized, bureaucratic, and finally infrastructural intelligence. As states became more complex, the demand for reliable information grew beyond informal networks. The world wars demonstrated the strategic value of codebreaking, deception, reconnaissance, and analysis, while the Cold War made intelligence permanent, global, technical, and deeply connected to ideology.

By the late twentieth century, intelligence had become part of the hidden infrastructure of modern states. It did not guarantee wise choices, but it meant that politics, war, and crisis were increasingly shaped by classified knowledge, secret assessments, and covert capabilities.

This history matters because it shows that today's agencies are not anomalies. They are the latest form of a long effort by states to reduce uncertainty and manage threats through secrecy. The next chapters examine the myths, failures, and controls that surround that hidden infrastructure.

Intelligence and Empire: Covert Operations, Corporate Interests, and Geopolitical Power

The history of secret services cannot be separated from the history of empire, because intelligence agencies often became instruments for defending geopolitical hierarchy, corporate access, and preferred political orders.

Intelligence services did not operate only at the boundary between rival states. During the Cold War, they also became instruments through which powerful states defended economic access, strategic influence, and preferred political orders abroad. Covert operations were often justified through the language of anti-communism and national security, but in practice they could also protect corporate interests, resource control, and geopolitical hierarchy.

Nowhere is this clearer than in a series of CIA-backed interventions in countries whose governments challenged Western economic or strategic priorities.

CIA and Regime Change: Guatemala, Iran, Chile, and the Pattern of Imperial Intelligence

The history of Cold War intelligence cannot be understood without examining how agencies such as the CIA often linked anti-communist strategy, geopolitical influence, and the protection of Western economic interests. Officially framed as defending "freedom" against communism, covert operations also targeted governments whose policies threatened Western corporate interests – particularly when those governments attempted land reform, nationalization of resources, or economic policies that prioritized local development over foreign ownership.

Guatemala 1954: Land Reform and United Fruit

The CIA-orchestrated coup against democratically elected President Jacobo Árbenz was not simply a response to Soviet aggression; Guatemala had limited Soviet ties. A central issue was Árbenz's land reform program, which expropriated unused land from the United Fruit Company, now Chiquita, to redistribute it to landless peasants. United Fruit had deep connections to the Eisenhower administration, and CIA Director Allen Dulles had previously been linked to the company.

Operation PBSUCCESS[3] combined propaganda, paramilitary training, aerial pressure, and psychological warfare to destabilize and ultimately overthrow Árbenz. The operation installed a military dictatorship that reversed land reform, returned property to United Fruit, and opened the way to decades of violence against Indigenous Mayans, leftist organizers, and other perceived opponents. The case shows how intelligence operations could serve economic and geopolitical interests when corporate property and regional influence were treated as matters of national security.

---

3. Operation PBSUCCESS was the CIA-backed covert operation that helped overthrow Guatemala's democratically elected president Jacobo Árbenz in 1954. Árbenz's land reform had affected the holdings of the United Fruit Company, and the coup installed a military regime that reversed the reforms and opened a long period of repression and civil conflict.

Iran 1953: Oil Nationalization as a Security Problem

Operation Ajax[4], which removed Prime Minister Mohammad Mossadegh, followed a similar logic. Mossadegh's central conflict with British and American interests lay in his decision to nationalize Iran's oil industry, threatening the position of the Anglo-Iranian Oil Company, later British Petroleum. British intelligence approached the CIA, framing oil nationalization as a development that could open space for Soviet influence.

The CIA helped organize propaganda, political pressure, payments to local actors, and coordination with military figures in a coup that restored the Shah's authority. For the next quarter-century, Western oil interests retained favorable access while the Shah's security apparatus, SAVAK, became notorious for repression. When Iranians overthrew the Shah in 1979, the revolution's anti-American character was shaped in part by the memory of foreign-backed intervention.

Chile 1973: Democratic Socialism and Covert Destabilization

Salvador Allende's[5] democratic election in 1970 on a platform of nationalizing copper, land reform, and socialist transformation threatened Chilean elites and important American corporate interests, including ITT and Anaconda Copper. The Nixon administration viewed Allende's government as both an ideological and strategic danger, and the CIA supported efforts to weaken his administration.

The CIA funded opposition media and parties, maintained contacts with military actors, supported destabilizing political efforts, and contributed to an

---

4. Operation Ajax was the 1953 CIA- and British-backed operation that helped overthrow Iranian Prime Minister Mohammad Mossadegh after his government nationalized Iran's oil industry. The coup restored the Shah's authority and became a lasting symbol of Western intervention in Iran's political and economic sovereignty.

5. Salvador Allende, a democratically elected socialist president of Chile, was overthrown in a military coup on 11 September 1973. General Augusto Pinochet then established a military dictatorship marked by repression, disappearances, torture, and neoliberal economic reforms. U.S. policy toward Allende's government remains one of the most debated examples of Cold War intervention in Latin America.

atmosphere of economic and institutional crisis. The 1973 coup led by Augusto Pinochet installed a regime responsible for mass repression and for radical market reforms that later became influential beyond Chile. The case illustrates how covert action could intersect with domestic polarization, corporate interests, and Cold War strategy.

A Recurring Cold War Pattern

These cases should not be treated as identical, nor as proof that intelligence agencies could simply manufacture history at will. Local elites, military factions, economic crises, ideological conflicts, and social divisions all mattered. Covert action did not create these conditions from nothing, but it could amplify them, finance certain actors, weaken elected governments, and shape moments of political crisis.

Taken together, Guatemala, Iran, and Chile suggest a recurring Cold War pattern: anti-communist language often provided the public justification for covert intervention, while geopolitical influence, corporate interests, and existing economic arrangements were also protected. In several cases, governments became targets not only because of their international alignments, but because their policies threatened foreign ownership, resource control, landholding patterns, or established economic power.

Similar dynamics appeared elsewhere, including in Congo, Brazil, Indonesia, Greece, Bolivia, Nicaragua, and El Salvador. The details differed, but the broader question remained: when intelligence agencies defined reformist, nationalist, socialist, or non-aligned governments as security threats, whose security was being protected, and whose political choices were being overridden?

Nicaragua and the Sandinistas: Revolution, Counterrevolution, and Covert War

The Sandinista Revolution in Nicaragua added another variation to this Cold War pattern. After the overthrow of the Somoza dictatorship in 1979, the Sandinista[6] government pursued land reform, literacy campaigns, social programs, and a foreign policy less dependent on Washington. To the Reagan administration, however, Sandinista Nicaragua was not treated primarily as a small country trying to reorganize itself after dictatorship, but as a strategic foothold for left-wing influence in Central America. U.S. support for the Contras – armed counterrevolutionary forces fighting the Sandinista government – showed how covert action could be used not simply to collect intelligence, but to weaken, destabilize, and pressure a revolutionary government whose political orientation challenged the regional order. The case also illustrates the blurred boundary between anti-communist security doctrine and the defense of geopolitical hierarchy: the question was not only whether Nicaragua posed a direct military threat, but whether an alternative model of development and sovereignty could be allowed to survive within the U.S. sphere of influence.

Intelligence, Resource Politics, and Contemporary Partnerships

In later decades, similar tensions appeared in intelligence partnerships with authoritarian regimes, especially where energy, mining, arms sales, migration control, counterterrorism, or regional influence were involved. The language changed from anti-communism to stability, counterterrorism, and strategic cooperation, but the underlying dilemma remained: intelligence cooperation can protect important security interests while also strengthening repressive governments or shielding unequal economic arrangements.

This does not mean every intelligence partnership is reducible to corporate extraction or imperial control. States do face real threats, and cooperation can sometimes prevent violence. But the historical record warns that "stability" is never a neutral term. It may mean protection from war or terrorism; it may also mean protection of regimes, contracts, resources, and geopolitical hierarchies. The central question is therefore not only whether intelligence cooperation serves security, but what kind of order it helps preserve.

Gladio: Imperial Intelligence Inside the NATO Bloc

Operation Gladio[7] was the codename commonly used for the Italian branch of a broader "stay-behind" system: clandestine networks set up in Western Europe after the Second World War, in cooperation with NATO and Western intelligence services, to organize armed resistance in case of a future Soviet invasion and occupation. In practice, these networks combined hidden weapons caches, secret communications channels, and pre-selected local contacts who could form the backbone of a guerrilla or clandestine organization operating behind enemy lines. From the outside they looked like a technical component of military preparedness; from the inside they raised deeper questions about secrecy, political alignment, and democratic control.

When we speak of "imperial intelligence", attention usually gravitates towards classic cases of external intervention: coups, covert operations, and hidden influence in states whose governments were seen as a threat to the strategic or corporate interests of great powers. In public imagination, these are CIA operations in Iran, Guatemala, Chile, or intelligence involvement in Latin America and other regions of the global South. Less visible, but conceptually just as important, are the cases where the logic of imperial intelligence is not applied "out there" on the periphery, but inside the alliance itself – in this case, within the NATO bloc. Operation Gladio and the broader stay-behind structures in Western Europe represent precisely this kind of phenomenon: a fusion of anti-communist doctrine, secret military-intelligence networks, and limited democratic oversight over a security infrastructure managed by both domestic elites and transnational alliance structures.

Stay-behind networks: between defense and a hidden infrastructure of power

The officially declared purpose of stay-behind networks was military-strategic. In the context of the Cold War and the fear of a possible Soviet attack on Western Europe, NATO and individual member states developed clandestine structures whose task was, in case of occupation, to provide the nucleus of resistance: hidden weapons depots, secure communication channels, logistical support, contacts in local communities, and pre-arranged networks of people ready to act as guerrillas or clandestine organizations. In this version of the story, stay-behind networks appear as an extension of normal deterrence and defense logic, relocated into the secret realm, outside visible military units and standard chains of command.

However, the very fact that such infrastructure is built in advance, in secrecy, and often with minimal or no sustained parliamentary oversight already raises questions that are central to understanding imperial intelligence. Who decides who belongs to these networks? According to which political criteria are individuals and organizations chosen and entrusted with access to weapons, resources, and sensitive information? To what extent does "resistance to future occupation" overlap with the interests of domestic elites in strengthening an anti-communist front, and with the interest of the transatlantic alliance in securing the political orientation of member states even in conditions of deep social change? In practice, stay-behind networks often leaned on right-wing, anti-communist, and nationalist milieus, which created a lasting asymmetry: the potential infrastructure of violence and secret organization sat much closer to one part of the political spectrum than to others.

This gap between the declared purpose (resistance to occupation) and the concrete social and political alignments (closeness to particular ideological environments) makes stay-behind networks relevant to the broader argument of this book. They show how "national security" in the Cold War framework easily intertwines with the preservation of a specific internal order and ideological orientation, not only with territorial defense against external invasion.

Gladio and the "strategy of tension": between documents and interpretation

In public debates, the name Gladio is most often used to refer to the Italian branch of stay-behind networks and the controversies surrounding its alleged role in waves of political violence and terrorist attacks from the 1960s to the 1980s. In that story, the concept of a "strategy of tension" appears – the idea that parts of the state apparatus, intelligence structures, and far-right groups allegedly used or tolerated violence in order to generate fear and polarization, delegitimize the left, and justify hard-line "security" policies. Over time, this narrative became a central axis of many conspiracy theories in which Gladio is portrayed as an almost omnipotent hidden hand, orchestrating terrorist attacks in order to manage democracy from the shadows.

That approach is problematic for at least two reasons. First, it homogenizes complex and often fragmentary historical episodes into a single, simple story about an all-powerful secret organization, pushing aside the role of local actors, political conflicts, social movements, economic crises, and open struggles for power. Second, it erases the difference between what is documented (the existence of stay-behind structures, links to NATO, certain connections to right-wing circles, specific failures and cover-ups) and what remains at the level of interpretation or suspicion (the degree of command, coordination, or conscious steering of particular acts of violence). That distinction is a central pillar of this book: drawing a clear line between archival facts, well-grounded but limited interpretations, and speculations that cross the boundaries of responsible analysis.

If we view Gladio through this lens, the focus shifts from the question "was a given operation centrally directed by a single hidden command?" to questions such as "what kind of power infrastructure was created by the fusion of secret networks, intelligence services, and alliance structures?" and "how did that infrastructure shape the range of possible political alternatives?". Even if we bracket the more radical claims about direct orchestration of violence, one fact remains: in some states there was a long-standing tradition of secret, anti-communist structures closely connected to parts of the military, the security apparatus, and the international alliance. Such a configuration of power by itself affects how "normal" politics is defined, which options are treated in advance as unacceptable, and how open democratic change of political direction really is.

Imperial logic inside the alliance: whose security is being protected?

Gladio and related networks show that imperial intelligence does not operate only in the form of relations between center and periphery, metropole and colony, or a great power and a "problematic" Third World state. It can also operate within formally equal alliances, through asymmetric control of information, techniques, doctrines, and secret structures. In the Cold War NATO framework this meant that key strategic assumptions – the communist threat, the need for permanent readiness, the legitimacy of preventive secret networks – originated in the alliance core, but were built into the internal security architecture of individual member states.

The result was a double loyalty of secret structures. Their nominal task was to protect the nation-state from future occupation, but they were simultaneously part of a broader imperial infrastructure of power whose parameters were defined at the level of the bloc rather than exclusively at the level of national parliaments and publics. In practice, this meant that decisions about the existence and functioning of certain networks were more exposed to alliance security perceptions than to open democratic debate within individual societies. When the existence of these networks became public in the late Cold War and post-Cold War period, parliamentary inquiries and public controversies in several European states showed precisely this: the surprise of elites who formally represented "national" politics when confronted with structures that had existed in their own backyard for decades, but outside their effective oversight.

This asymmetry leads directly to a question that runs through the entire book: whose security is actually being protected? In the case of stay-behind networks, the answer is not straightforward. There is, without doubt, an element of genuine strategic concern about a Soviet invasion and occupation scenario. At the same time, the choice of partners, the criteria of trust, and the political horizon within which these networks were conceived reveal a clear anti-communist, anti-left, and pro-Atlantic frame. Such a frame does not only defend physical territory from a hypothetical military threat; it also protects a particular reconstruction of the political and economic order in post-war Europe: a certain model of liberal capitalism, a certain version of social democracy that does not cross systemic boundaries, and certain foreign-policy orientations that remain within alliance parameters.

Seen from this angle, imperial intelligence in the case of Gladio is a fusion of three levels of power. The first is military-strategic: preparation for the scenario of invasion and occupation. The second is domestic-political: securing an anti-communist, status-quo orientation in the internal political field. The third is transnational: maintaining NATO cohesion through clandestine infrastructural networks that connect services, militaries, and selected social actors across borders. One does not have to accept the most radical conspiratorial narratives to see that such a configuration of power shapes democratic imagination – what counts as a legitimate change and what is marked as a dangerous deviation that may trigger "security" reflexes.

Mossad and the Architecture of Imperial Intelligence

Mossad is often described through legendary operations and images of surgical efficiency, but it is more useful to see it as a pillar of a broader security state. Its mandate and methods are inseparable from a political order marked by permanent conflict, entrenched inequality, and a far-reaching security economy. The service does not merely collect secrets or neutralize threats; it helps define who counts as a threat, whose lives are protected, and which forms of violence are treated as normal instruments of statecraft.

In this sense, Mossad condenses several themes central to imperial intelligence: the projection of power beyond borders, the blurring of war and peace, and the use of covert action to stabilize a particular regional order. Intelligence is not just a passive mirror of danger; it is an active tool of shaping the environment in which danger is produced, interpreted, and managed.

Myth, Justice, and Selective Memory

Public narratives about Mossad emphasize emblematic operations: the capture of Adolf Eichmann in Argentina, the pursuit of those responsible for the Munich massacre, and covert actions to bring endangered Jewish communities to Israel. These stories anchor a powerful moral image of the service as an agent of historical justice, an avenger of past atrocities, and a guardian of a vulnerable people.

Yet the same state that sent agents after Nazi criminals also cultivated close security and military relations with authoritarian regimes, including governments responsible for systematic racism and repression. Intelligence cooperation, arms deals, and technology transfers sat alongside rhetoric about human rights and historical trauma. The contrast is instructive. It shows how heroic episodes, however real, can function as legitimating islands in a wider archipelago of practices that serve strategic interests rather than universal principles.

In the framework of imperial intelligence, such myths are not accidental. They provide a moral vocabulary that helps normalize permanent exceptional measures: targeted killings, extraterritorial operations, and a broad definition of security that extends far beyond immediate self-defense.

Targeted Killings and the Normalization of Exception

Mossad's reputation is closely tied to targeted assassinations, kidnappings, and sabotage operations abroad. These acts are rarely acknowledged directly, but they follow a recognizable pattern. High-profile opponents of the state are killed or disappear; foreign police and media reconstruct the operation; the government maintains a posture of studied ambiguity. Responsibility is understood, but seldom confessed.

This ambiguity performs a legal and political function. It keeps actions in a grey zone, where formal accountability is hard to attach yet deterrent and symbolic effects are achieved. The state assumes the right to exercise lethal force far beyond its borders, outside declared war, on the basis of internal designations of threat. Intelligence services design and implement these operations with minimal external oversight, while public narratives reframe them as precise, necessary, and morally distinct from the violence of others.

Imperial intelligence operates precisely in such spaces of exception. The tools it uses–covert action, deniable force, clandestine influence–are justified as unique responses to unique dangers. Over time, however, they become normalized; the extraordinary becomes routine. When that happens, the distinction between protecting lives and projecting power blurs, and the category of "legitimate target" can quietly expand.

Mossad Within a Broader Regime of Control

Mossad is one agency among several, alongside domestic security services and military intelligence. Together, they sustain a dense infrastructure of surveillance, management, and coercion that extends from occupied territories to distant diasporas. Intelligence is not only about foreign enemies; it is woven into the regulation of a stratified social order.

Monitoring of Palestinian activists, students, and organizations, both locally and abroad, fits into a wider practice of fragmenting and pre-empting opposition. Pressure on international officials, judges, or investigators who seek to scrutinize state conduct illustrates another dimension: the use of intelligence capabilities against legal and diplomatic challenges. Covert influence, leaks, intimidation, and reputational campaigns become tools for shaping the space in which accountability is even thinkable.

From the standpoint of imperial intelligence, this is characteristic. The same apparatus that manages threats at the borders also manages the boundaries of permissible criticism. Intelligence power is deployed not only against armed groups, but also against journalists, NGOs, and multilateral institutions that try to impose common rules on the use of force.

Security, Technology, and Exporting Expertise

The service is also embedded in a security-technology complex that transforms conflict into expertise and expertise into commodity. Techniques developed for surveillance, targeting, and social control in one theatre of conflict are repackaged as "solutions" for other states' problems: border control, urban unrest, migration management, counter-insurgency. The line between intelligence and industry becomes porous.

This dynamic is central to the contemporary form of imperial intelligence. Knowledge and tools circulate through networks of allies, arms clients, and security partners. A sensor field tested on one population is marketed to governments on other continents. Databases and algorithms prototype on specific groups inform broader trends in policing and social management. Mossad is not the commercial actor in this chain, but it contributes to the reservoir of practices and doctrines that underpin it.

In effect, a particular model of security governance–rooted in permanent alert, risk scoring, and pre-emptive action–travels outward. States that adopt its tools also absorb aspects of its logic. Intelligence, in this sense, becomes both a mechanism and an ideology: a way of seeing the world in which prevention justifies expansion and secrecy shields asymmetries of power.

Failure, Blind Spots, and the Limits of Control

Moments of dramatic failure expose the limits of this model. The surprise achieved by the 7 October 2023 attack[8] –despite extensive technical surveillance and a dense informant network–revealed not only gaps in data processing but deeper blind spots. A security system that assumes a besieged population is ultimately controllable may discount evidence that does not fit that assumption. Apparent stability can be misread as consent or fatigue rather than as a pause before eruption.

Imperial intelligence is especially vulnerable to such blind spots because it sits close to power and often shares its premises. When the basic political architecture is taken as given, intelligence work tends to focus on tactical disruptions and operational risks, not on cumulative structural pressures. The result can be an apparatus that knows a great deal about individuals and networks, and far less about the conditions that make those networks multiply.

For Mossad, as for other services, this creates a paradox. The stronger and more technologically sophisticated the apparatus becomes, the easier it is to believe that every problem has a security solution. When that belief fails, the consequences are borne not only by institutions but by civilians on all sides.

---

8. The Hamas-led assault on southern Israel on 7 October 2023 began with a large rocket barrage from Gaza and was followed by armed incursions into Israeli territory, including attacks on kibbutzim, towns, military positions, and the Nova open-air music festival near Re'im. Around 1,200 people were killed in the wider attack, and about 250 were taken hostage into Gaza. The scale, coordination, and surprise of the assault, despite Israel's extensive intelligence, surveillance, and border-control systems around Gaza, made it a major example of contemporary intelligence and security failure.

Myths and Realities

After every major shock, the myths return. A government falls, a terrorist attack succeeds, a protest movement grows, or a scandal appears–and the public imagination searches for the hidden hand behind the visible event.

The appeal is understandable. Secret services operate behind closed doors; their documents are classified, their methods concealed, and their failures often discovered only after damage has been done. Secrecy creates silence, and silence invites stories.

These myths are dangerous because they flatten reality. They either turn services into supernatural forces or reduce every secret institution to the same machinery of control. Both views make it harder to ask the practical questions: what can these agencies actually do, where do they fail, who controls them, and under what rules?

When Myth Replaces the Archive: 9/11 in the Public Imagination

The 9/11 attacks[1] quickly entered popular culture and conspiracy discourse as the archetype of a perfectly orchestrated operation that was "too big to miss," in which secret services either knew everything and deliberately stayed silent, or even helped stage the events from within. In films, books, and online forums, it is often implied that such an attack could not have happened without "inside help," so every inconsistency, contradictory statement, or procedural mistake is read as proof of hidden orchestration rather than as the kind of confusion that typically accompanies a major crisis.

Publicly available investigations – from the 9/11 Commission Report to congressional and expert inquiries – draw a more mundane but in many ways more disturbing picture: warning signals scattered across different agencies, poor information-sharing between the FBI, CIA, and other bodies, systematic underestimation of Al-Qaeda's capabilities, rigid procedures, and cognitive frames that imagined terrorism mostly through "classic" scenarios rather than as hijacked airliners turned into weapons. Instead of a single hidden design, the archival record shows institutional inertia, weak coordination, and flawed assumptions that created the space the attackers exploited. That gap between myth and documentation lies at the core of this book.

What Secret Services Can and Cannot Do

Because secret services operate out of public view and fiction has made them familiar symbols of hidden power, they attract stories that exaggerate both their competence and their menace. Understanding them requires separating those stories from institutional reality.

---

1. The attacks of 11 September 2001 were coordinated al-Qaeda attacks against the United States, involving hijacked commercial airplanes used against the World Trade Center and the Pentagon, while a fourth plane crashed in Pennsylvania. In intelligence studies, 9/11 is often analyzed as a failure of collection, sharing, analysis, warning, and interagency coordination, and it led to major changes in U.S. security and surveillance law.

Myth 1: Secret services are all-powerful and everywhere

The first great myth is that secret services see everything and can intervene anywhere. In this view, no serious plot can escape them and no event is beyond manipulation: if something happens, "they" allowed it or arranged it.

Reality is different. Intelligence agencies have significant capabilities, but they face hard constraints: coverage gaps, legal and practical limits, finite processing capacity, unreliable human sources, deception, language barriers, secure communications, and the sheer scale of global activity.

Access becomes power only when information is interpreted well, communicated clearly, and used responsibly.

Myth 2: Secret services always know the truth; politicians simply hide it

A related myth assumes that intelligence agencies possess "the truth" and that politicians merely hide it. In this view, full disclosure of secret reports would end confusion and settle debate.

In practice, intelligence offers assessments, not pure certainty. It works with incomplete and sometimes contradictory information, caveats, confidence levels, and alternative explanations. Uncertainty is not a defect of intelligence; it is part of the reality intelligence tries to manage.

Politicians can suppress, exaggerate, or selectively use intelligence, but that does not mean a single clear truth sits hidden inside the files. Even within agencies, analysts often disagree about what the evidence shows.

When We Assume "The Services Know Everything": 9/11 and the Investigation Commissions

In the years since 11 September 2001, a persistent belief has taken hold in parts of the public: that intelligence services "knew everything" about the coming attacks but chose not to act, or were blocked by political leaders who preferred to let the catastrophe happen. This narrative appears in many conspiracy accounts as a simple explanation for a complex failure: if the attacks were not prevented, it must be because someone at the top wanted them to succeed. Every prior warning, missed lead, or bureaucratic mistake is then retroactively reinterpreted as proof of deliberate inaction rather than as evidence of a system struggling with its own limitations.

Official investigations, however, tell a different and more complicated story. The 9/11 Commission concluded that the core problems were "failures of imagination, policy, capabilities, and management," not the existence of a single, clear picture that was cynically ignored. Its report highlighted fragmented responsibilities across multiple agencies, a culture of "need to know" that discouraged information-sharing, weak analytical capacities in key organizations, and chronic information overload that made it hard to distinguish critical signals from background noise. Separate reviews of the FBI's performance reached similar conclusions, describing "significant systemic problems" in how intelligence was handled, insufficient strategic analysis, and poor internal dissemination rather than a conscious decision to suppress clear warnings.

These findings do not absolve institutions or leaders. They show that responsibility lay in system design and management, not in a simple story of services choosing not to act. The claim that "they knew everything" erases cognitive bias, bureaucratic friction, and political uncertainty–the very mechanisms that make intelligence failure possible.

Myth 3: Every major event has a hidden "hand of the services"

Another myth claims that no major event is spontaneous. Revolutions, protests, crashes, elections, terrorist attacks, even disasters are attributed to secret services. Suspicion replaces analysis: if an outcome is important, it must have been engineered.

This way of thinking confuses influence with control. Intelligence agencies do sometimes intervene in political processes: they may support certain actors, spread information or disinformation, or conduct covert operations. They may help shape the environment in which events unfold. Yet revolutions, elections, crises, and wars also depend on local actors, institutions, economies, social pressures, accidents, and timing.

Belief in a universal hidden hand feeds conspiracy culture. It offers a simple explanation for complex events, turning history into a story of perfect planners and powerless populations. It removes the role of error, accident, unintended consequences, and ordinary political struggle.

The danger is that one myth turns politics into conspiracy, while another turns secrecy into trust. A mature view must hold influence and constraint, necessity and danger, secrecy and accountability together.

The Myth of an Omnipotent CIA: Iran 1953 and Chile 1973

The CIA's role in the 1953 coup in Iran and the 1973 coup in Chile has shaped the agency's image as an engineer of regime change. In Iran, Operation Ajax helped remove Prime Minister Mohammad Mossadegh and restore the Shah's authority; in Chile, the CIA supported anti-Allende forces, funded opposition media and parties, and maintained contacts with actors who destabilized the government before the military coup. These cases show real covert influence, not imaginary power.

The archival record also shows contingency. In Iran and Chile, the CIA operated within local crises shaped by domestic elites, military factions, economic pressure, ideological conflict, and social polarization. Covert action mattered, but it did not create history from nothing. It amplified forces already present.

These cases show that the CIA can significantly influence conditions and outcomes, especially when local structures are already fragile. At the same time, they simplify history if they are read as proof that one external actor can topple any government at will. Iran 1953 and Chile 1973 demonstrate the dangers of secret power in foreign policy, but they also reveal how much even a strong intelligence service depends on local conditions, allies, timing, resistance, and uncertainties it can never fully command.

Myth 4: Democratic and authoritarian services are essentially the same

A fourth myth claims that democratic and authoritarian services are basically the same: every state uses secrecy to control society, while laws and oversight merely provide decoration.

This view misses structural differences. In democracies, agencies are at least formally bound by legislation, courts, specialized authorization procedures, parliamentary committees, watchdogs, and public controversy. These safeguards are imperfect, but they create friction, documentation, and avenues of challenge that authoritarian systems usually suppress.

These mechanisms are imperfect. Democracies have experienced serious scandals involving illegal surveillance, political misuse of intelligence, and rights violations. But the presence of independent institutions and public debate makes it possible, in principle, to challenge, correct, and constrain secret services.

In authoritarian and totalitarian regimes, by contrast, intelligence and security organs often operate as core instruments of regime power. They may have broad or vague mandates, minimal legal constraints, and no meaningful oversight. Their primary mission is to protect the ruling group, not to serve the public interest. Surveillance, harassment, imprisonment, torture, and enforced disappearance can become routine tools. Citizens have little recourse against abuses, and secrecy serves to protect perpetrators rather than to defend legitimate security needs.

To say that democracies and dictatorships are "the same" in this regard erases these differences and undermines the importance of legal and institutional safeguards. It also feeds cynicism that benefits those who wish to weaken oversight and accountability. Recognizing that intelligence work is intrinsically risky does not require ignoring the real distinctions between systems.

Why Myths Arise: Secrecy, Gaps, Fiction, and Propaganda

First, secrecy encourages imaginative explanation. When citizens know that important institutions operate out of sight, they speculate about what those institutions might be doing. Myths fill gaps with stories that feel coherent, even when they are poorly supported.

Second, popular culture thrives on dramatic stories. Films, novels, and series rarely show analysts wrestling with ambiguous data or committees debating legal constraints. They show daring agents, perfect gadgets, and decisive conspiracies because those make for better entertainment. Over time, fictional tropes bleed into public expectations. The real work of intelligence, with its bureaucracy, uncertainty, and partial successes, can seem dull by comparison, and the gap is filled with cinematic imagination.

Third, political actors have incentives to manipulate perceptions of secret services. Governments may play up intelligence successes to reinforce their image of competence, or blame intelligence failures for policies that went wrong. Opposition groups may invoke hidden manipulation to delegitimize governments or explain their own defeats. Foreign states use propaganda to portray rival services as either incompetent or fearsome, depending on the message they want to send.

Finally, conspiracy narratives offer psychological comfort. They turn a messy world into one governed by hidden planners, reducing helplessness and avoiding the harder work of understanding social, economic, and political complexity.

What Secret Services Can Actually Do

Clearing away myths does not minimize the real power of secret services. They can intercept communications, recruit insiders, run covert operations, access classified information, reveal hidden threats, map hostile networks, and provide early warning. In wartime and crisis, good intelligence can save lives and prevent escalation.

Secret services can also shape how leaders see the world. The assessments they produce influence decisions about war and peace, sanctions and diplomacy, internal security and foreign intervention. An agency that systematically overestimates or underestimates a threat can push policy in more aggressive or more complacent directions. An agency that is politicized can become a tool for justifying predetermined choices.

Moreover, intelligence and security organs in repressive systems can directly affect the everyday lives of citizens. Surveillance, blackmail, arbitrary detention, and violence can be used to silence dissent, enforce conformity, and maintain fear. Even in democracies, excessive or unlawful surveillance can chill free expression and erode trust in institutions.

Their work is shaped by practical obstacles: adversaries adapt and deceive, technical systems fail, human sources mislead, and data overload can be as dangerous as data scarcity.

Analysis is further constrained by cognition and organizational culture. Assumptions, preferred narratives, groupthink, and confirmation bias can prevent agencies from recognizing looming threats or fundamental shifts.

In democracies, law, oversight, courts, and public scrutiny can restrict intrusive methods and make abuse riskier. In authoritarian systems, formal limits are weaker, though services still face resources, rivalries, and the need to keep society functioning.

Disarming the Myths

Exaggerated stories distort public debate: benign myths encourage complacency about secrecy and power, while myths of total hidden control encourage fatalism and conspiracy thinking.

The more useful question is therefore not whether secret services are strong or weak in the abstract, but how particular institutions behave in particular political, legal, and technological settings.

Why Intelligence Fails

Intelligence failures are usually recognized too late. Before the event, the evidence is scattered, ambiguous, and easy to explain away. After the event, the same evidence appears painfully obvious. A warning that once seemed vague becomes a missed alarm. A report buried in a file becomes the crucial clue. A hesitation that once looked reasonable becomes negligence. Hindsight turns fragments into a pattern, and the public asks the question that follows almost every catastrophe: how could they not have known?

But intelligence failure rarely begins with total ignorance. More often, it begins with partial knowledge: a signal noticed but not shared, a source believed too late, a pattern hidden inside too much data, an assumption that no one challenges, a warning softened until it loses urgency, or a political leader unwilling to hear what the evidence suggests. Failure grows in the spaces between institutions, inside habits of thought, and around decisions that seem defensible at the time.

To understand failure, we must look beyond the comforting idea of one decisive mistake. Failure usually emerges from a chain: collection gaps, processing delays, analytic bias, bureaucratic rivalry, weak warning, political pressure, and the refusal or inability to act.

Errors, Bias, Politics, and Organizational Friction

Intelligence services are often judged by their failures. The question "Where were the services?" is sometimes fair, but it often rests on a misunderstanding: failure is a built-in risk of intelligence work, not an exceptional accident.

This chapter looks inward, at the cognitive, organizational, and political forces that make failure possible even in well-resourced systems.

Types of Intelligence Failure

Intelligence can fail at every stage of the cycle described earlier. A basic typology helps clarify where things go wrong.

Failure to collect

Sometimes agencies simply do not have the information they need. They may lack sources in crucial places, be blind to certain communication channels, or be technologically outmatched. Potential agents may refuse recruitment; key systems may be too well protected; adversaries may use unexpected methods. In such cases, the gap is not in analysis but in access: the necessary raw material never arrives.

Failure to share

Even when information exists somewhere in the system, it may not reach those who need it. Different agencies may each hold fragments of a critical picture but fail to combine them. Classification barriers, mutual distrust, incompatible databases, and bureaucratic rivalries can all prevent timely sharing. In some cases, an agency may deliberately withhold information to protect sources, methods, or turf.

Failure to process

Information that is technically collected can still be lost in practice if processing systems are overloaded or poorly designed. Massive inflows of data may outstrip the capacity to sort, translate, decrypt, and index. Important signals can be buried in noise, misclassified, or simply not reviewed in time. This type of failure is particularly acute in the digital age, where volume itself is a problem.

Failure to analyze

Analysts may misinterpret or misprioritize the information they have. They can misjudge which indicators matter, dismiss crucial warnings, or fail to consider plausible alternative explanations. They may also cling to outdated models of an adversary's behavior and fit new data into old narratives, rather than letting narratives adjust to data.

Failure to warn

Sometimes analysts understand that a threat is real and growing but fail to express their concerns in a way that grabs the attention of decision-makers. Warnings may be buried in routine reports, hedged so heavily with caveats that urgency is lost, or delivered to the wrong audience at the wrong time. In other cases, repeated warnings can lead to "warning fatigue," causing leaders to discount yet another alarm.

Failure to act

Finally, even clear and accurate warnings can fail if decision-makers do not act. Leaders may calculate that responding would be too costly, politically risky, or disruptive. They may hope that a problem will resolve itself, or they may be distracted by other priorities. In such cases, the failure lies not in the intelligence system but in the political system's willingness or ability to respond.

"Connecting the Dots": 9/11 as a Chain of Failure

The attacks of 11 September 2001 are often described as a failure to "connect the dots," but that phrase can sound deceptively simple. In reality, 9/11 was not the result of one missing clue or one negligent official. It was the product of a long chain of failures stretching across collection, information-sharing, analysis, warning, and policy response. The 9/11 Commission later summarized the broader picture as a set of failures of "imagination, policy, capabilities, and management," a formula that remains useful because it captures both the abundance of available signals and the institutional inability to turn them into effective preventive action.

At the level of collection, the problem was not the total absence of warning. Before 9/11, the U.S. government already knew that al-Qaeda had carried out major attacks, including the 1998 embassy bombings in East Africa and the attack on the USS Cole in 2000, and intelligence reporting repeatedly indicated that Osama bin Laden sought to strike inside the United States. Foreign governments, clandestine reporting, and U.S. intelligence streams all contributed fragments suggesting a dangerous and evolving threat. Inside the United States, some operational clues also existed, including suspicious travel patterns, extremist connections, and later-discovered leads involving future hijackers. The issue was therefore not that nothing had been collected, but that relevant information existed in scattered, incomplete, and unevenly valued pieces.

The next link in the chain was fragmentation and incomplete sharing. The 9/11 Commission found major barriers between the CIA, FBI, and other parts of the government, reinforced by institutional cultures, legal uncertainty, and the long-standing "need to know" principle. Information about some future hijackers, including Khalid al-Mihdhar and Nawaf al-Hazmi, did not move effectively from the CIA to the FBI even after intelligence officials had reason to know that they had entered the United States. Reviews of FBI handling of intelligence similarly pointed to weak procedures for documenting and acting on information received from other agencies, especially when that information arrived informally rather than through clear, standardised channels. In such a system, no single institution possessed the entire picture, and no mechanism reliably assembled the relevant fragments into one operational warning.

Processing and analysis added another layer. Agencies were not simply short of information; they struggled to sort large volumes of partial, ambiguous, time-sensitive reporting. Familiar analytic narratives shaped what seemed plausible, and bureaucratic routines diluted urgency.

At the warning stage, some signals reached political leadership but not in a form that triggered decisive disruption. The 6 August 2001 President's Daily Brief, "Bin Ladin Determined to Strike in US," showed concern about al-Qaeda's intentions, but it did not provide operational details that could easily be turned into immediate preventive action.

The failure was therefore not one dramatic moment in which leaders ignored a complete picture. The system failed to convert strategic awareness into urgent, coordinated action.

The post-hoc investigations are important because they show where the chain broke and why simplistic conspiracy explanations are so misleading. The 9/11 Commission did not conclude that the U.S. government possessed a complete picture and deliberately suppressed it. Instead, it identified systemic weaknesses: poor information-sharing, fragmented authority, inadequate counterterrorism architecture, weak domestic intelligence capabilities, and a broader failure to imagine the form of the threat. Related reviews of FBI performance added more specific operational problems, including weak documentation practices, limited analytic integration, and unclear responsibilities when intelligence moved across agency lines. In this sense, 9/11 is the paradigmatic modern intelligence failure: not a case of total ignorance, but of partial knowledge that never became usable collective understanding.

Cognitive Bias: How Minds Misread the World

Analysts are human beings. They interpret information through mental frameworks shaped by experience, training, and culture. These frameworks help them make sense of complex data, but they also introduce predictable distortions known as cognitive biases.

Confirmation bias

Confirmation bias is the tendency to seek, notice, and value information that supports existing beliefs more than information that challenges them. Once analysts form a view–about a regime's stability, an adversary's intentions, or the likelihood of a threat–they may unconsciously give more weight to data that fits that view and rationalize away conflicting evidence. Over time, this can turn a working hypothesis into an unexamined assumption.

Mirror-imaging

Mirror-imaging occurs when analysts assume that others think and act as they themselves would in similar circumstances. They project their own values, risk calculations, and decision styles onto foreign leaders or organizations. This can be misleading when dealing with actors who have different strategic cultures, historical experiences, or ideological commitments. What seems irrational or unlikely from one perspective may be entirely plausible from another.

Groupthink

Groupthink arises when teams of analysts, managers, or inter-agency committees value consensus and harmony over critical debate. Dissenting views may be discouraged, marginalized, or self-censored. Early assumptions harden into orthodoxy, and contradictory evidence is seen as an annoyance rather than a signal. Under groupthink, intelligence products may appear confident and unified while actually resting on fragile foundations.

Other biases–such as availability (overestimating the importance of recent or vivid events), anchoring (being overly influenced by initial information), and optimism or pessimism biases–can also affect judgments. Training and structured analytic techniques can mitigate, but not eliminate, these tendencies. The point is not that analysts are uniquely flawed; it is that their work must confront uncertainty while using minds that naturally prefer coherence.

When a Threat Seems Unthinkable: The Yom Kippur War, 1973

On the eve of the Yom Kippur War in October 1973, Israel possessed substantial intelligence capabilities directed at its main adversaries, Egypt and Syria. It had technical collection on Arab military deployments, human sources in key positions, and years of experience analyzing regional crises. Yet, despite mounting indicators that both states were preparing for coordinated action, Israeli intelligence and political leadership remained convinced that a large-scale attack was highly unlikely. This gap between growing warning signs and entrenched expectations is often described as a "conceptual failure": the danger was visible in the data, but it did not fit the dominant mental model of what Egypt and Syria were likely to do.

At the core was "the Concept": the belief that Egypt would not launch a major war until it could strike deep into Israeli territory and neutralize Israeli air superiority, while Syria would not move without Egypt. This framework made the Arab build-up appear coercive or defensive rather than as preparation for war.

As a result, a series of specific warnings failed to shift the prevailing view. Intelligence reports indicated unusual Egyptian and Syrian movements, the evacuation of Soviet dependants, and the forward positioning of Egyptian forces and bridging equipment along the Suez Canal. Individual analysts and some senior officers became increasingly uneasy, but their concerns were weighed against the established assessment that Arab leaders would not risk war without clear air superiority. In internal debates, the burden of proof effectively lay with those arguing that war was imminent, not with those defending the status quo assumption. The same data that, in a different conceptual context, might have been read as a dangerous pattern was instead repeatedly explained away as signalling or bluff.

The Yom Kippur War shows that intelligence can fail even when services possess information. Israel saw much of the military preparation, but interpreted it through a rigid framework that made attack seem unlikely. Warning indicators were present; the conceptual lens made them less persuasive.

Organizational Weaknesses: Rivalry, Silos, and Inertia

Even if individual analysts were perfectly rational, intelligence organizations would still face structural problems. Large bureaucracies create their own obstacles to clear thinking and effective action.

Rivalry and silos

Different agencies may compete for influence, resources, and prestige. Each may guard its sources and methods, reluctant to share because sharing might diminish its distinct value. Over time, this can produce "silos" where information and expertise are trapped within institutional boundaries. An agency may see only part of a problem and resist integrating its view with others'.

Poor coordination

Joint bodies, task forces, and coordination committees are designed to overcome fragmentation, but they do not always work as intended. Lines of authority may be unclear. Meetings may become ritualistic rather than substantive. Time pressures can push participants toward lowest-common-denominator positions. Systems for sharing data may be technically incompatible or administratively cumbersome.

Bureaucratic inertia

Organizations develop routines and standard operating procedures. These can be efficient when situations are familiar, but they can become liabilities when the environment changes. Requests for new approaches may be slowed by layers of approval. Proposals that challenge existing structures may be seen as threats. Units that were created to address one type of threat may struggle to adapt when the nature of danger shifts.

Incentives and career dynamics

The internal incentive structures of intelligence organizations also matter. If careers are built by avoiding mistakes rather than by asking hard questions, analysts may become risk-averse and reluctant to challenge prevailing views. If promotions depend on producing products that match what superiors or political leaders want to hear, independent judgment suffers. If failures are punished harshly but successes are taken for granted, the safest course may be to remain within comfortable assumptions.

These organizational forces can turn what should be a self-correcting system into one that reinforces its own blind spots. Even when individuals see problems, they may find it difficult to shift institutional behavior.

Politicization: When Intelligence and Power Collide

Intelligence and politics are inevitably connected. Intelligence exists to inform political decisions, and political leaders set priorities for intelligence work. But this relationship can become distorted in two directions: political influence over intelligence and intelligence influence over politics.

Politics pressuring intelligence

Politicization in one sense occurs when leaders pressure agencies to produce assessments that support preferred policies. They may signal, explicitly or implicitly, what conclusions are desirable and what will be unwelcome. They may reward compliant officials and marginalize those who present inconvenient evidence. Over time, this can create a culture in which analysts self-censor or unconsciously slant their judgments to align with leadership expectations.

In such environments, intelligence failures are not simply mistakes; they are structured outcomes. Agencies may downplay emerging threats because acknowledging them would undermine a cherished policy. They may overstate dangers to justify aggressive actions. The boundary between analysis and advocacy blurs.

Intelligence failure usually reveals wider institutional weakness: agencies that do not question assumptions, analysts pressured toward comfortable conclusions, bureaucracies that do not share information, and leaders who prefer confirmation to warning. Reducing failure requires stronger analytic tradecraft, better information-sharing, protected dissent, honest post-crisis review, and a political culture willing to hear bad news.

The Iraq War 2003: Intelligence Under Political Pressure

The U.S. and British decisions to invade Iraq in 2003 on the grounds that Saddam Hussein possessed weapons of mass destruction (WMD) have become a textbook example of how intelligence can be drawn into a political project. Pre-war assessments, especially the U.S. October 2002 National Intelligence Estimate and British Joint Intelligence Committee papers, judged with high confidence that Iraq retained chemical and biological weapons and was pursuing nuclear capabilities. Subsequent investigations – in particular the U.S. Senate reports, the Robb-Silberman Commission, and the British Hutton and Butler inquiries – concluded that these judgments were "almost entirely wrong," but they also revealed a more complex pattern than a simple story of fabricated intelligence.

At the analytic level, intelligence on Iraqi WMD was thin, dated, and dependent on defectors and indirect sources. Analysts filled gaps with worst-case assumptions drawn from Saddam's past behavior, previous WMD programs, and efforts to evade inspections, while dissenting views were often less visible in public presentation.

Politicisation appeared less as direct orders to falsify intelligence than as a pattern of framing, selection, and sharpening. Nuanced judgments became more certain in political speech, while doubts and caveats receded.

In public discourse, analytic nuance and political messaging drifted apart. Leaders presented active WMD stockpiles and programs as near-certain, often citing intelligence more firmly than the underlying assessments justified.

Intelligence pushing politics

Conversely, intelligence services can try to shape politics. Senior intelligence officials may use their perceived authority and access to secrets to influence public debate or policy choices. They may leak selected information to the media to weaken opponents or strengthen allies. In extreme cases, intelligence organizations may become semi-independent power centers, seeking to steer the state rather than merely inform it.

Both forms of politicization undermine the credibility and effectiveness of intelligence. When analysis becomes a tool of policy rather than a check on policy, decision-makers lose the ability to see the world as it is rather than as they wish it to be. When intelligence officials see themselves as political players, public trust in secret institutions erodes.

Three Common Patterns of Failure

The themes above often crystallise into recurring patterns. Three are particularly important.

Case Sketch 1: Missing the Unthinkable

One common pattern of failure involves threats that seem "unthinkable" before they happen. Prior to a major surprise attack or sudden collapse of a regime, signals may be visible: unusual movements, changes in communication, hints from sources, or rising tensions. Yet these signals do not fit prevailing assumptions about what the adversary would dare or desire to do. Analysts and leaders find it hard to imagine that a drastic move is really coming.

In such cases, collection may be adequate–information exists–but analysis and warning fail. Cognitive bias leads to discounting extreme possibilities; groupthink discourages those who raise alarm; bureaucratic caution makes it difficult to escalate concerns. When the unthinkable happens, the failure is described as a lack of imagination, but it is also a product of institutional comfort with existing narratives.

Case Sketch 2: Seeing Only What Politics Wants to See

Another pattern arises when a government is committed to a particular policy–such as war, intervention, or partnership–and intelligence is expected to support that policy. Agencies collect and analyze, but assessments that question the policy's premises meet resistance.

Warnings about unintended consequences, local dynamics, or the fragility of allies may be softened, delayed, or buried. Threats that justify the chosen course are highlighted; evidence that challenges it is treated skeptically. Over time, the intelligence picture presented to leaders, parliaments, and the public becomes skewed. When the policy fails, the record shows that some within the system raised doubts, but their voices never shaped the official narrative.

Here the failure is not purely technical or cognitive; it is political. The intelligence system's function as an independent check on policy has been compromised. What looks from the outside like "bad intelligence" is often, from inside, a story of pressure, incentives, and selective hearing.

Case Sketch 3: Drowning in Data, Starving for Insight

In the digital era, some of the most striking errors arise not from a lack of information but from its excess. Agencies collect enormous quantities of data: communications metadata, intercepted content, sensor streams, open-source feeds. Many potential indicators of a threat are already present in the system, but they are scattered across databases, poorly linked, or lost in the noise.

Analysts and automated tools may flag individual items, but without effective integration, patterns remain invisible. Resource constraints and processing limits force triage; some leads are not pursued. Different units may assume that "someone else is responsible." When a terrorist attack or cyber operation succeeds, post-event investigations often reveal that relevant data existed, but the system failed to turn it into timely, actionable insight.

These examples highlight that intelligence failure can stem precisely from success in collection. The challenge is no longer just to capture signals, but to design organizations and tools that can filter, connect, and interpret them without being paralysed by their sheer volume.

Failure as a Systemic Risk, Not Just Betrayal

Public reactions to intelligence failures often look for villains: a traitor who leaked secrets, a lazy official who ignored a report, a single agency that "failed to connect the dots". Although sabotage and gross negligence do occur, most major failures are systemic. They arise from the interplay of human bias, organizational culture, bureaucratic structure, technological limits, and political context.

Recognizing this has two implications. First, it cautions against simplistic reforms based only on punishing individuals or rearranging boxes on organizational charts without addressing deeper issues. Second, it reminds us that some level of failure is inevitable. Intelligence services operate under uncertainty, against adversaries who adapt and deceive. They will never achieve perfect foresight.

That does not mean, however, that failure should be accepted passively. On the contrary, improving intelligence requires simultaneous work on multiple fronts: diversifying sources and perspectives, encouraging dissent and alternative analyses, building robust mechanisms for sharing data, designing better processing systems, protecting analysts from undue political pressure, and cultivating leaders who value uncomfortable truths.

Intelligence failure is rarely only a story of treason or incompetence. More often, it reveals where systems, incentives, assumptions, and channels of communication have broken down. Studying failure is therefore not only a matter of assigning blame; it is a way of seeing how secret institutions can become more rigorous, less biased, and more honest about uncertainty.

Selective Attention: Far-Right Violence and the Surveillance of the Left

Intelligence agencies in liberal democracies fail to prevent far-right terrorist violence while maintaining extensive surveillance of left-wing movements. This asymmetry reveals priorities.

In Germany, the Verfassungsschutz (domestic intelligence) failed to detect or stop the National Socialist Underground (NSU), a neo-Nazi terror cell that murdered at least ten people between 2000-2007–despite having paid informants inside the group. Meanwhile, the same agency devoted significant resources to monitoring anti-fascist activists and left-wing organizations.

Critics have argued that U.S. security agencies have often underestimated the threat of far-right violence while devoting significant attention to Black Lives Matter, environmental activists, and Muslim communities. Internal FBI documents obtained through FOIA requests have been cited in support of this concern, especially after the Bureau used “Black Identity Extremism” as a domestic threat label. For critics, this asymmetry suggests that intelligence failure is not always a neutral absence of knowledge; it may also reflect institutional assumptions about which groups are treated as dangerous and which threats are minimized.

These are not random failures–they reflect institutional cultures shaped by class and racial hierarchies. Far-right violence often targets marginalized communities (immigrants, Muslims, Black people, Jews) whose security is lower priority than protecting property and social order. Far-right ideology is compatible with capitalist social relations; left-wing movements challenge them.

When intelligence "fails" to stop fascist violence but "succeeds" in disrupting environmental or labor movements, this reveals what these institutions actually protect.

Secret Services, Law, and Freedom

A secret service is born from fear, but it must not be allowed to rule through fear. Every society faces real dangers: attacks that must be prevented, spies who must be discovered, networks that must be understood, and crises that cannot be handled only by public institutions working in the open. For that reason, even free societies accept a difficult bargain: some institutions may operate in secrecy, use intrusive methods, and see things ordinary citizens are not allowed to see.

But the same bargain contains a danger. The power to watch can become the power to intimidate. The power to collect information can become the power to destroy reputations, pressure opponents, or control public life. A file opened for security reasons can become a political weapon. A surveillance measure justified by threat can become a habit of governance. What begins as protection of the state can slowly turn into protection of those who control the state.

The decisive question, therefore, is not whether secret services should exist, but what prevents them from crossing the line. Law can define their powers, but law without oversight becomes decoration. Oversight can restrain them, but oversight without access to truth becomes theatre. Freedom depends not on trusting secret institutions blindly, but on building rules strong enough to make secrecy serve the public rather than the regime.

From Security to Political Police

Intelligence and security services exist because states face real threats. Terrorist attacks, espionage, sabotage, cyber intrusions, and violent extremism can cost lives, destabilize institutions, and undermine the basic conditions of a functioning society. In this sense, the existence of secret services is not, by itself, an anomaly.

Most citizens accept that some specialized institutions must operate partly in secrecy to protect them from dangers that cannot be managed in the open.

But the same powers that make secret services effective–surveillance, infiltration, data collection, covert operations–also make them inherently dangerous to freedom. The line between protecting a constitutional order and controlling a population is thin and easily crossed. The central question is therefore not only *what* secret services do, but under what rules, for whose benefit, and with what limits.

Legitimate Security: Intelligence Under Law

In a democratic constitutional framework, the legitimate function of secret services is to protect the state and its citizens from serious threats within a clear legal mandate. Their purpose is not to shape politics or manage public opinion, but to provide decision-makers with information about risks and to support law enforcement, defense, and crisis management.

Three principles are central to this model.

First, legality. Intelligence and security services must operate within laws that define their mandates, powers, and limits. Those laws should specify what types of threats justify intrusive measures, what procedures must be followed to authorize them, and what oversight mechanisms exist. Secret operations may be classified, but the basic rules governing them should not be.

Second, necessity and proportionality. Intrusive powers–interception of communications, covert searches, surveillance of individuals or groups–should be used only when necessary to address a genuine threat and only to the extent proportionate to that threat. This implies a preference for less intrusive methods when they are sufficient and for time-limited measures tailored to concrete risks rather than open-ended monitoring.

Third, purpose. The use of intelligence powers should be linked to the protection of identifiable public interests such as national security, public safety, or the integrity of democratic institutions. They should not be used to advantage particular parties, leaders, or private interests. When services begin to serve political goals unrelated to their mandate, they drift away from legitimate security and toward political policing.

In practice, these principles are not self-enforcing. They require institutions and norms that keep services answerable to law rather than to the convenience of rulers.

From Security to Political Police: When the Line Is Crossed

Political police emerge when intelligence and security organs systematically target individuals and groups not because they pose genuine threats to public safety or constitutional order, but because they are perceived as political, social, or ideological opponents of those in power. Instead of focusing on acts of violence, espionage, or sabotage, political police focus on loyalty and conformity.

This transformation can be gradual. It often begins with the expansion of the category of "security threat." Opposition parties, critical journalists, civil society organizations, religious communities, minority groups, or student movements are recast not as legitimate participants in public life but as potential subversives. The language changes: dissent becomes "extremism," criticism becomes "destabilization," organizing becomes "foreign interference."

Surveillance of such actors is justified by vague or flexible notions of national security. Files are opened on individuals not because they have committed or planned crimes, but because they might "influence" others or "create unrest." Informants are recruited not to prevent violence but to map networks of association. Intelligence reports are used to discredit opponents, control appointments, or intimidate critics.

Over time, this logic can produce a system in which entire social sectors–universities, media, civil society, professions–live with the knowledge that they may be watched, recorded, and punished for stepping outside permitted lines. Fear becomes a central method of governance. In extreme forms, such as totalitarian regimes, secret police create dense webs of informers, maintain detailed dossiers, and use arrest, torture, and disappearance to enforce obedience.

Political police are not defined only by brutality, but by their underlying purpose: they protect the ruling regime rather than the constitutional order or the community of citizens it is meant to serve.

Democratic Models: Law, Limits, and Oversight

Democratic systems cannot eliminate the risks inherent in secret power, but they can design frameworks that reduce them and provide mechanisms for correction. Several elements are characteristic of such frameworks.

Clear legal mandates

Intelligence and security agencies should be established by law, with mandates that define their areas of responsibility–foreign intelligence, domestic security, military intelligence, technical collection–and their relationship to other institutions. Laws should specify the types of threats they may address and the methods they may use, leaving as little room as possible for open-ended interpretation.

Authorization and warrant procedures

Intrusive powers typically require authorization beyond the agency itself. Courts, special judges, or independent commissions may be empowered to approve surveillance, searches, or other measures, ensuring that there is an external check before rights are restricted. In urgent situations, powers may be used with retroactive review, but such exceptions should be narrowly defined.

Proportionality and time limits

Democratic legal frameworks often require that intrusive measures be proportionate to the threat and limited in duration. Surveillance on a particular target must be justified by specific grounds and periodically renewed only if those grounds persist. Broad, indiscriminate surveillance of entire populations is more difficult to reconcile with these principles, which is why it has sparked intense debate in many democracies.

Parliamentary and independent oversight

Legislative committees, ombuds institutions, inspectors general, and specialized oversight bodies review the activities of secret services. They may examine compliance with law, investigate complaints, audit operations, and issue reports. Their effectiveness depends on access to information, technical expertise, and political will. When oversight is weak or partisan, laws on paper may matter little.

Transparency and public debate

While operational details must remain secret in many cases, democracies benefit from public debate about the general scope and direction of intelligence policies. Declassification of historical records, publication of legal frameworks, and disclosure of oversight reports–at least in redacted form–help citizens understand how secret powers are used. Free media and civil society can raise alarms when abuses surface.

These mechanisms are far from perfect. Democracies have experienced illegal surveillance of activists, overbroad collection of communications data, cooperation in abuses abroad, and other violations. But the presence of independent courts, journalists, and political competition creates conditions under which abuses can be exposed and, at least sometimes, corrected. The gap between democratic ideals and practice is often wide; yet the ideals themselves serve as tools for critique and reform.

Authoritarian Models: Fear, Files, and Regime Protection

In authoritarian and totalitarian systems, the relationship between secret services, law, and freedom is fundamentally different. Intelligence and security organs tend to act as pillars of regime control rather than as neutral protectors of public safety.

Law as instrument, not constraint

Where laws exist, they are often vague, broad, or easily overridden. Emergency powers can be declared indefinitely. Security organs may be granted authority to act on "suspicion" or to protect "state security" without clear definitions. Courts are subordinated to the executive or party structure, and oversight bodies, if they exist, lack independence or coercive power.

Surveillance as social control

Monitoring of citizens extends well beyond genuine threats to include political opponents, independent media, civil society organizations, religious groups, and marginalized communities. Surveillance is used not only to prevent specific acts, but to create a climate in which people censor themselves. The knowledge or perception that "someone may be watching" shapes behavior, discouraging collective action.

Files and blackmail

Authoritarian security services often maintain extensive files on individuals, documenting political views, personal vulnerabilities, family ties, and compromising behavior. These files can be used to block careers, co-opt individuals, or coerce cooperation. The boundary between intelligence, gossip, and blackmail disappears.

Repression and violence

In more extreme forms, secret police practice arrest, torture, and extrajudicial killing. Suspected opponents can be detained without trial; confessions extracted under duress; families intimidated. Abductions, disappearance, and targeted killings may be used at home or abroad. The purpose is not only to neutralize specific individuals but to send signals that deter others.

Protection of the regime

Above all, authoritarian intelligence and security organs serve the ruling regime or party. They may involve themselves in managing elites, preventing defections, and mediating internal conflicts. They protect the leadership from coup attempts and popular uprisings. They may also engage in propaganda and disinformation to shape perceptions at home and abroad.

While authoritarian systems can be highly repressive, they are not always efficient or stable. Overlapping agencies may compete; corruption may spread; fear may yield false information as people say what they believe interrogators want to hear. But the direction of accountability is clear: services answer upward to the regime, not outward to the public.

Freedom depends not only on whether secret services formally obey rules, but on who defines those rules and who can challenge their violation. A democratic system is free when limits can be tested, enforced, debated, and revised in the open. The boundary between security and political policing is therefore not secrecy itself, but accountability.

Why Even Strong Oversight Has Structural Limits

The previous sections outlined how parliamentary committees, judicial review, independent commissioners, and internal controls can constrain intelligence power in democratic systems. These mechanisms matter. They create friction, impose procedural requirements, expose some abuses, and provide legal tools for challenging unlawful surveillance. A critical analysis, however, must also recognize their structural limits. Oversight can reduce harm and correct particular abuses, but it does not automatically resolve the deeper political question of what intelligence agencies are built to protect, how threats are defined, and whose interests are treated as part of "national security."

Class Composition and Shared Assumptions

Parliamentary intelligence committees, judicial panels reviewing surveillance warrants, and independent oversight commissioners are usually drawn from political, legal, administrative, and security establishments. They are rarely rooted in the communities most affected by surveillance: workers' organizations, racialized minorities, anti-war groups, environmental movements, migrant communities, or other groups that have historically been monitored as potential sources of disorder.

This does not mean that all oversight actors are dishonest or consciously biased. The problem is more subtle. Oversight institutions operate within the same political and legal culture that defines certain forms of property, order, and state authority as normal, while treating some forms of disruption as security risks. When intelligence agencies monitor labor militancy, environmental direct action, anti-capitalist organizing, or radical social movements, oversight bodies may examine whether procedures were followed without fully questioning the broader framing that made such movements appear as threats in the first place.

Historical examples illustrate this difficulty. When COINTELPRO[1] operations targeted the Black Panther Party and other movements, later investigations treated those actions as serious abuses requiring reform. That exposure mattered. Yet the broader tendency to classify radical challenges to racial, economic, or imperial power as security concerns did not disappear; it reappeared under different legal categories and institutional vocabularies.

The Secrecy Problem

Oversight bodies themselves often operate under conditions of secrecy. Parliamentary committees hold classified hearings; judicial review may occur in closed proceedings; independent commissioners often issue reports with sensitive details removed. Some secrecy is unavoidable when sources, methods, and ongoing operations are involved. But secrecy also limits democratic evaluation.

Citizens usually cannot know what questions were asked, what information was withheld, which trade-offs were accepted, or whether oversight bodies challenged agencies forcefully enough. This can produce a gap between the formal existence of oversight and the public's ability to judge its effectiveness. The public sees institutions designed to check secret power, but much of their actual work remains invisible.

This invisibility matters. When oversight bodies warn that surveillance is excessive, the strongest details may remain classified. When they approve expansive programs, the reasoning may be inaccessible. The result is not that oversight is meaningless, but that its democratic value depends heavily on how much information can eventually be disclosed, how independent the overseers are, and whether civil society, journalists, courts, and whistleblowers can test official claims from outside the classified system.

Threat Construction and Captured Discourse

Intelligence agencies often control much of the information that reaches oversight bodies. They decide what to classify, what to declassify, which threats to emphasize, and how to describe the risks attached to particular targets or movements. This gives agencies significant influence over the narrative environment in which oversight takes place.

Overseers may see intercepts suggesting a possible plot, assessments warning of radicalization, or reports describing activism as a public-order concern. They may see less of the ordinary political organizing being monitored, the nonviolent movements being disrupted, or the corporate and state interests indirectly protected by those operations. When agencies frame labor strikes as threats to critical infrastructure, Indigenous land defense as extremism, or anti-war mobilization as a security concern, oversight bodies may struggle to challenge those categories unless they have independent sources of information and a wider understanding of social conflict.

This is one of the central weaknesses of oversight: it often reviews intelligence work through categories created by the intelligence system itself. Oversight can ask whether procedures were followed, whether warrants were obtained, and whether legal thresholds were met. It is much harder for it to ask whether the original definition of the "threat" was politically distorted.

Revolving Doors and Cultural Capture

Oversight can also be weakened by shared professional cultures. Former intelligence officials may advise oversight bodies; members of oversight committees may later move into security, defense, or private intelligence roles; and specialized oversight often requires security clearances and insider knowledge. These relationships can create familiarity, trust, and expertise, but they can also reduce the willingness to confront agencies aggressively.

The problem is not only corruption or personal loyalty. It is cultural capture: the gradual internalization of the assumptions, language, and priorities of the security world. What agencies describe as "reasonable," "necessary," or "operationally sensitive" can become the common sense of oversight itself. The very expertise needed to supervise intelligence services may also make overseers more dependent on the institutions they are meant to scrutinize.

Legal Frameworks and Their Limits

Judicial oversight operates within legal frameworks that define what counts as a threat, what standards justify surveillance, and which rights may be limited in the name of security. Courts can impose important constraints, especially when they require warrants, proportionality, evidence, and time limits. But courts usually do not redesign the political assumptions built into security law.

When judges review surveillance requests, they often apply categories such as terrorism, espionage, extremism, organized crime, or foreign interference. These categories may be necessary in some cases, but they can also expand or blur. Political organizing can be reframed as extremism; protest can be described as disorder; disruption of business operations can be treated as a threat to critical infrastructure. Even strong judicial oversight may therefore fail to challenge the deeper question of whether security law itself has been stretched to protect established power.

Why This Matters for Reform Strategies

Recognizing the structural limits of oversight does not mean abandoning efforts to strengthen it. Parliamentary committees with real investigative powers, independent commissioners who can compel testimony, whistleblower protections, public reporting requirements, and judicial review all matter. They can slow the expansion of surveillance, expose specific abuses, create legal tools for challenging unlawful targeting, and preserve institutional memory of past violations.

But these gains are limited and reversible. Oversight can restrain intelligence agencies, but it cannot by itself democratize the social order in which they operate. If the broader political system treats labor disruption, anti-capitalist organizing, racial justice movements, or environmental resistance as threats to order, then oversight may review the legality of surveillance without fully confronting its political purpose.

The point is therefore not that oversight is useless. It is that oversight must be paired with broader democratic pressure: public debate, investigative journalism, legal challenges, whistleblower protection, social movements, and a wider redefinition of security around human needs rather than only state stability or economic order.

The Dual Task

For citizens navigating intelligence power in democratic societies, the task is therefore dual.

Tactically, citizens should demand stronger oversight within existing systems: greater transparency, better parliamentary access, stronger judicial standards, independent commissioners with real powers, meaningful whistleblower protections, and public reporting wherever possible. These measures can protect vulnerable communities, expose abuse, and create space for democratic resistance.

Strategically, citizens should also recognize that procedural reforms cannot solve every structural problem. Intelligence agencies operate within societies marked by inequality, class power, racial hierarchy, geopolitical conflict, and corporate influence. Lasting change therefore requires more than technical improvements to oversight. It requires democratic movements capable of challenging how security itself is defined, who gets protected, who gets monitored, and whose interests are treated as the public interest.

FISA and the PATRIOT Act[2]: How the Legal Framework Shifts After Shock

The terrorist attacks of 11 September 2001 triggered a rapid and far-reaching expansion of surveillance powers in the United States, framed as a necessary response to a new kind of threat. The Foreign Intelligence Surveillance Act (FISA), originally adopted in 1978 to regulate secret surveillance targeting foreign

2. The Foreign Intelligence Surveillance Act (FISA) of 1978 created a legal framework and a special court for approving certain national-security surveillance activities in the United States. The USA PATRIOT Act, passed after the 11 September 2001 attacks, expanded investigative and surveillance powers, including broader information sharing, roving wiretaps, and easier access to certain business and financial records.

powers and their agents, had already created a specialized court (the FISA Court[3]) to review government applications for national-security wiretaps and searches. After 9/11, Congress moved quickly to loosen some of these constraints and to extend the reach of national-security surveillance into new domains, particularly through the USA PATRIOT Act, passed in October 2001.

One key legal change concerned the boundary between foreign-intelligence collection and ordinary law enforcement. Before 2001, FISA required that the "purpose" of surveillance be foreign intelligence; the PATRIOT Act lowered this to a "significant purpose," giving agencies more flexibility to share information between intelligence and criminal investigations.

The PATRIOT Act also broadened surveillance tools: roving wiretaps, easier access to business and financial records, and longer duration for some FISA orders. Together, these measures expanded the speed, scale, and reach of security investigations.

The post-9/11 evolution of FISA and the PATRIOT Act thus highlights the enduring tension between security and liberty in democratic responses to shock. On one side stands the argument that extraordinary dangers require broader, more flexible powers and faster information-sharing; on the other, the concern that changes adopted in crisis moments become normalised, allowing long-term intrusions into the lives of ordinary citizens with limited transparency or oversight. The American experience since 2001 shows how quickly legal obstacles to surveillance can be lowered in the name of preventing another catastrophe, and how difficult it can be, once the immediate fear has faded, to restore a balance that gives equal weight to rights and to security.

The Central Question: To Whom Are Services Accountable?

The differences between democratic and authoritarian models can be summarized in one simple question: *To whom do secret services ultimately answer?*

---

3. The Foreign Intelligence Surveillance Court is a specialized U.S. court that reviews government applications for certain forms of national-security surveillance. Its proceedings are usually secret, which has made it central to debates about whether classified judicial oversight can provide meaningful accountability.

In a democracy, they are supposed to answer to the constitution, the law, and, through elected representatives and independent institutions, to the people. Their powers are justified by reference to public interests, and their legitimacy depends on remaining within boundaries set by law and overseen by bodies that are not controlled by the agencies themselves.

In authoritarian systems, secret services answer primarily to the ruling leadership–whether a single person, a party, or a narrow elite. Law, where it exists, is subordinate to political will. Oversight, where it exists, is subordinate to the regime. The agencies' legitimacy is defined by their effectiveness in maintaining power, not by their respect for rights.

Even within democracies, this question remains active. Periodic scandals remind citizens that agencies can drift toward serving narrower interests if oversight weakens or if fear is used to justify ever-expanding powers. The temptation to treat political opponents as security threats is never fully absent. Conversely, in some hybrid or transitional regimes, formal democratic structures coexist with powerful security organs that still behave like political police.

Recognizing these dynamics gives citizens a normative compass. When intelligence powers are used transparently within law, to address specific and serious threats, under real oversight, they can be compatible with freedom. When they are used broadly against lawful dissent, shielded from scrutiny, and justified by vague appeals to security, they become tools of domination.

If rules on surveillance apply only to formal state agencies, while the same effect is achieved by purchasing or acquiring data from private intermediaries, then the core purpose of the law – protecting citizens from the state's unlimited gaze – is undermined, even when the letter of the law is formally respected. Normatively serious regulation of intelligence work in the digital era must therefore treat state services and infrastructural private actors as a functional whole: what endangers the citizen is not only "the service" itself, but the entire constellation of institutions and markets that makes it possible for their behavior to be continuously recorded, linked, and evaluated.

The challenge is not to decide once and for all whether secret services are "good" or "bad," but to examine the conditions that direct their power. Law, institutional design, political culture, and civic vigilance all matter. Secret services will likely remain part of the hidden machinery of modern states; what matters is who watches them, under what rules, and in whose name. These questions lead directly to the institutional problem of oversight: if secret services are necessary but dangerous, who can meaningfully supervise them?

Oversight and Accountability

A DEMOCRACY DOES NOT lose its freedom only when tanks appear in the streets or elections are openly abolished. Sometimes the erosion is quieter. A surveillance power is expanded after a crisis. A secret interpretation of the law becomes routine. A parliamentary committee receives polished briefings but never the documents that matter. A journalist discovers abuse only years after it began. A citizen suspects they have been watched, but cannot prove it, challenge it, or even learn which institution was responsible.

This is the central difficulty of controlling secret power: the agencies that most need oversight are often the hardest to see. They operate behind classification rules, national security exemptions, covert methods, foreign partnerships, and technical systems that few outsiders fully understand. The public is asked to trust institutions whose work it cannot directly inspect. Parliaments, courts, inspectors, journalists, and civil society are asked to hold power accountable while much of the evidence remains hidden.

Oversight exists to make that impossible task at least partly possible. It does not mean revealing every source, operation, or method. It means ensuring that secrecy does not become a blank cheque. It means creating enough independent access, legal authority, expertise, and public reporting to prevent secret services from becoming laws unto themselves. The question is old, but in the age of mass surveillance and secret legal interpretations it has become sharper than ever: who watches the watchers?

Who Watches the Watchers?

Secret services are granted extraordinary powers: to intercept communications, to monitor suspects, to run covert operations, and to handle information that ordinary citizens never see. Without such powers, states would struggle to detect and prevent serious threats. But with such powers, intelligence and security agencies can easily overreach, abuse rights, and drift toward serving narrower interests than the public good. Oversight and accountability are therefore not luxuries or optional extras. They are essential components of any state that wants to combine security with freedom.

Oversight asks a simple but demanding question: *who watches the watchers?* The answer is not one institution but a network of mechanisms–formal and informal, internal and external–that together shape how secret services behave.

Types of Oversight: Multiple Lines of Control

Different systems use different combinations of oversight, but several broad types recur in democracies.

Legislative (parliamentary) oversight

Parliaments or legislatures often establish specialized committees to oversee intelligence and security services. These committees may review budgets, examine policy frameworks, scrutinize major operations after the fact, and question agency leaders. In some countries, they have access to classified information and can publish reports, sometimes in redacted form. Their effectiveness depends on their legal powers, political independence, and ability to work across party lines.

Judicial oversight

Courts or special judicial bodies may be required to authorize intrusive measures such as wiretaps, searches, and certain surveillance activities. They can review whether interventions are lawful, necessary, and proportionate. In some systems, individual complaints about rights violations can lead to judicial review of intelligence practices. Judicial oversight adds a layer of legal scrutiny that is external to the agencies and the executive.

Executive oversight

Ministers, presidents, or prime ministers, together with their staff and advisory councils, oversee intelligence as part of their responsibility for national security. They approve priorities, authorize certain operations, and can order internal inquiries. Executive oversight is crucial because intelligence agencies formally belong to the executive branch. But it can be double-edged: the same leaders who supervise agencies may also be tempted to misuse them.

Independent oversight bodies

Some democracies have created independent institutions–inspectors general, ombuds offices, or dedicated intelligence oversight commissions–tasked with auditing agency compliance with law and policy. These bodies may have legal powers to access documents, inspect facilities, and receive complaints. They can issue reports and recommendations, sometimes with binding force, sometimes only with moral and political weight.

Internal controls

Within agencies, internal affairs units, compliance offices, and legal advisers monitor adherence to rules. They review the legality of proposed operations, investigate misconduct, and provide guidance. While internal controls are not a substitute for external oversight, they can catch problems early and foster a culture in which rules are taken seriously rather than treated as obstacles to be evaded.

COINTELPRO and the Church Committee: Exposing Systemic Repression, Institutionalizing Limited Reform

In the early 1970s, a break-in at an FBI office in Media, Pennsylvania, exposed what many activists had long known but could not prove: U.S. intelligence and security agencies had conducted systematic operations against civil rights groups, anti-war activists, Black liberation movements, Indigenous organizations, labor unions, and left-wing political parties. The FBI's COINTELPRO programs, running from 1956 to 1971, infiltrated, harassed, and sought to "neutralize" these movements using covert and often illegal methods: surveillance, psychological pressure, fabricated documents, anonymous threats, wrongful imprisonment, and, in some cases, cooperation with local police actions that produced deadly consequences.

COINTELPRO was not simply a case of bureaucratic overreach. According to the Senate's own findings, the FBI's stated motivation included "protecting national security, preventing violence, and maintaining the existing social and political order." That formulation is revealing. It shows how national security could be defined broadly enough to include not only the prevention of violence, but also the protection of an existing political and social order from movements that challenged it. When civil rights organizers, Black liberation movements, anti-war activists, and labor organizers contested racial hierarchy, militarism, or corporate power, they were often interpreted not merely as political actors, but as potential threats to stability.

The tactics employed reveal the depth of this institutional logic. The Bureau did not simply monitor these groups; it worked to weaken and disrupt them through psychological operations, informants, forged documents, attempts to create internal conflict, coordination with local police, and other covert methods. Techniques developed for counterintelligence were applied to domestic social movements, treating political organizing as if it belonged in the same category as hostile subversion.

The Church Committee, established in 1975 after these revelations could no longer be ignored, documented extensive abuses: surveillance of Martin Luther King Jr. and other political figures, assassination plots against foreign leaders, bulk communications collection through programs such as Operation SHAMROCK, and CIA domestic spying. Over sixteen months of hearings, the Committee exposed intelligence agencies operating with limited oversight, broad secrecy, and expansive definitions of national security.

Crucially, the Church Committee framed these activities as abuses: serious deviations from lawful and legitimate intelligence work. That framing mattered because it made reform possible. Congress established permanent intelligence oversight committees and passed the Foreign Intelligence Surveillance Act (FISA) in 1978, creating legal procedures for surveillance and a specialized form of judicial review.

These reforms mattered in practice. They created procedural hurdles, increased transparency in limited ways, and provided institutional spaces where future abuses could be challenged. But they did not resolve the deeper problem: intelligence agencies have often been used to protect state authority and existing economic arrangements, especially when social movements are interpreted as threats to order. FISA courts have frequently approved surveillance requests, oversight committees often operate within the same security vocabulary as the agencies they supervise, and some COINTELPRO-like methods have reappeared under different legal and investigative frameworks.

The Church Committee therefore illustrates a recurring pattern in democratic systems: scandal exposes abuse, reform introduces new constraints, but the underlying tension between security, secrecy, and political power remains. Without pressure from journalists, civil society, courts, whistleblowers, and social movements, even limited reforms are unlikely to occur. Yet later controversies – from mass surveillance to counterterrorism operations targeting Muslim communities and the monitoring of racial justice or environmental movements – suggest that intelligence systems can adapt their methods without fully abandoning broad conceptions of security.

The lesson is not that oversight is meaningless. Legal constraints, public scrutiny, and institutional review can limit abuses and create space for resistance. But reform born from scandal is never a finished project. It cannot by itself resolve the deeper question of what social order intelligence institutions are designed to protect, how they define threats, and whose security is treated as the public interest.

Weak Oversight in Practice: When Parliament Lacks the Tools

On paper, many democracies have parliamentary committees tasked with overseeing intelligence services. In practice, these bodies may have limited access, weak capacity, and little expert support. A committee that receives thousands of classified pages days before a hearing, without technical staff or power to compel documents, formally oversees but substantively depends on the services it should scrutinize.

Legal and practical obstacles reinforce this weakness. Classification rules may prevent committee members from seeing key documents or from sharing concerns with colleagues and the public, even when they suspect that something is wrong. Governments can limit what information is provided, citing national security and ongoing operations; resource constraints mean that the committee cannot commission independent audits or investigations, and political dynamics often discourage confrontation with powerful security institutions. As a result, potential abuses – from disproportionate use of special surveillance measures to problematic cooperation with foreign services – remain hidden unless an insider leaks information, a whistleblower comes forward, or journalists manage to piece together a story from scattered sources.

This "silent failure" of oversight is less dramatic than open confrontation, but it has far-reaching consequences. When parliaments lack the tools, expertise, and political will to exercise meaningful control, the real checks on intelligence services shift elsewhere – to chance disclosures, court cases, or international pressure – and democratic accountability becomes reactive rather than proactive. Problems are then addressed only after scandals break, instead of being prevented or corrected early through steady, informed parliamentary scrutiny.

Public oversight: media, civil society, and whistleblowers

Although they do not see operational details, journalists, researchers, non-governmental organizations, and whistleblowers play a crucial role in exposing abuses and stimulating reform. Investigative reporting has uncovered unlawful surveillance, torture, political misuse of services, and secret cooperation with foreign agencies. Civil society campaigns have pushed for new laws and stronger oversight institutions. Whistleblowers–whether from inside agencies or from contractors–have sometimes revealed systemic problems, though often at great personal cost.

These forms of oversight are most effective when they reinforce each other. A parliamentary committee may rely on leaks or investigative journalism to know where to focus. Courts may respond to cases brought by civil society organizations. Independent bodies may push internal compliance units to act on patterns they see.

What Makes Oversight Effective?

Not all oversight is equal. It is possible to have impressive structures on paper that do little in practice. Several conditions determine whether oversight is genuinely effective.

Access to information

Oversight bodies cannot evaluate what they cannot see. They need legal authority and practical means to access relevant documents, databases, and personnel. Agencies may be reluctant to share sensitive material; laws must therefore grant oversight institutions the right to demand it, with narrow exceptions. Without this, oversight risks becoming a superficial formality.

Timeliness and tempo

Oversight must operate at a tempo that matches the work of the agencies. If reviews come only years later, issues may become entrenched before they are detected. While some oversight is necessarily retrospective, mechanisms should also provide for near-real-time monitoring of certain activities, especially those with serious rights implications.

Expertise and continuity

Intelligence work is technically and legally complex. Oversight bodies need members and staff with sufficient expertise to understand technical systems, legal frameworks, and operational realities. High turnover, lack of training, or reliance on part-time members can weaken their capacity. Continuity matters: long-serving staff who accumulate knowledge can spot patterns and avoid being misled by carefully curated presentations.

Political independence and will

Oversight institutions must be sufficiently independent from the agencies and from short-term political pressures. If their leadership is chosen purely along partisan lines, they may turn into instruments of political theater rather than genuine scrutiny. Even with good laws, oversight fails when key actors lack the will to confront powerful agencies, challenge popular narratives of security, or expose politically embarrassing abuses.

Transparency of findings

While operational details must often remain secret, the general findings of oversight bodies should be made public whenever possible. Publishing reports–redacted where necessary–creates external pressure for reform, informs public debate, and helps build trust that agencies are not operating without control. Secrecy about oversight itself undermines its legitimacy.

Follow-up and enforcement

Oversight is not only about discovering problems but also about ensuring that they are addressed. Recommendations need mechanisms for follow-up, and serious violations must trigger consequences–legal, administrative, or political. Without enforcement, oversight can devolve into mere advice that agencies are free to ignore.

When these conditions are present, oversight can shape agency behavior, deter abuse, and improve performance. When they are absent, oversight risks serving as a decorative shield, invoked to reassure the public while leaving underlying practices unchanged.

Oversight in the Age of Mass Surveillance and Secret Law[1]

The digital era has introduced new challenges for oversight and accountability. Mass surveillance capabilities–bulk data collection, metadata analysis, algorithmic sorting, and long-term retention of digital traces–have expanded what intelligence agencies can do. At the same time, the legal frameworks governing these practices have sometimes become more opaque.

Scale and complexity

Traditional oversight mechanisms were often designed for targeted operations: individual wiretaps, specific searches, discrete investigations. Mass surveillance changes the scale. Instead of authorizing intrusion into a single person's communications, authorities may authorize bulk collection affecting millions. Oversight bodies must therefore grapple with program-level questions: how systems operate, how data is filtered, who has access, how long information is stored, and how safeguards are implemented.

---

1. "Secret law" refers to classified legal interpretations, court decisions, or executive rules that shape how surveillance powers are actually used, while remaining unavailable to the public. The problem is not only that operations are secret, but that the legal meaning of public statutes may also be secretly expanded.

Secret law and secret interpretations

In some systems, legal justifications for surveillance programs, or official interpretations of existing laws, have been kept secret. Courts may issue classified opinions; internal legal memos may redefine what is "reasonable" or "proportionate" without public debate. This creates a gap between what citizens think the law allows and what agencies and executives believe it allows. Oversight bodies may be aware of these interpretations, but their ability to challenge or publicize them can be limited.

Technological asymmetry

Oversight institutions often lag behind agencies in technical capacity. Intelligence services employ engineers, cryptographers, data scientists, and cyber specialists. Oversight bodies may struggle to recruit or retain comparable expertise, making it difficult to interrogate technical claims or understand the implications of complex systems. Without technical literacy, oversight risks becoming over-dependent on agency explanations.

International cooperation

Intelligence is heavily transnational. Agencies share data, access each other's collection systems, or route operations through foreign partners. This can create oversight loopholes: what is prohibited domestically may be accessed via a foreign service; data subject to certain protections in one jurisdiction may be stored or processed in another with weaker rules. National oversight mechanisms are often not designed to monitor cross-border intelligence exchanges.

Addressing these challenges requires updating oversight practices and institutions. Technical expertise must be strengthened. Legal frameworks must be clarified and made as transparent as possible. International cooperation between oversight bodies may need to mirror, in some form, the cooperation between intelligence agencies. Above all, societies must decide how much intrusive capability they are willing to accept in exchange for security, and under what safeguards.

Examples of Strong and Weak Oversight

Comparative experience across democracies shows a wide range of oversight models, with varying degrees of success.

In some countries, parliamentary committees enjoy broad powers to access classified information, summon agency heads, and commission special inquiries. Independent commissioners or inspectors general conduct systematic audits of surveillance practices, review compliance with law, and issue public reports. Courts play an active role in reviewing warrants and in adjudicating challenges brought by individuals or organizations. These systems are not immune to failure, but they provide multiple points at which abuse can be detected and corrected.

In other democracies, oversight is more limited. Parliamentary committees may have narrow mandates or lack security clearances. Courts may defer heavily to executive claims of necessity or lack jurisdiction to review intelligence activities at all. Independent bodies may exist on paper but lack staff, authority, or political support. In such environments, major problems often surface only through leaks, scandals, or external pressure.

Historical episodes illustrate both sides. Revelations of unlawful domestic surveillance, secret cooperation in torture, or bulk collection of communications data have led some democracies to strengthen oversight: tightening legal standards, enhancing the powers of independent bodies, and increasing transparency about surveillance policies. In other cases, initial outrage has faded without substantial reform, leaving oversight structures largely unchanged.

The lesson is that oversight is not a static achievement. It must be maintained, renewed, and adapted as technologies and threats evolve. Periodic crises can be opportunities to improve controls, but they can also be moments when fear is used to justify expanding powers faster than oversight can catch up.

Oversight as a Pillar of an Intelligent State

The metaphor of intelligence services as the "hidden hand" of the state can be misleading if it suggests that secret agencies stand above or outside the constitutional order. In a genuinely intelligent state–one that learns, adjusts, and respects its own principles–oversight and accountability are fundamental, not peripheral.

Without oversight, secret services may be efficient in the short term but brittle in the long term. Abuses erode public trust, fuel conspiracy narratives, and delegitimize necessary security measures. Information becomes distorted by political pressure. Rather than clarifying reality for decision-makers, intelligence begins to echo their preconceptions.

With robust oversight, secret services can better serve their core purpose: reducing uncertainty about genuine threats in a way that is compatible with rights and the rule of law. Oversight does not guarantee perfection, but it creates incentives for honesty, restraint, and learning. It makes it more likely that agencies will admit mistakes, correct course, and resist becoming tools of partisan or personal power.

Who watches the watchers? In a healthy system, the answer is: many different actors, operating through different mechanisms, with overlapping responsibilities and mutual checks. A democracy is tested not only by the skill of its intelligence services in confronting danger, but by the strength of the institutions that keep those services tied to law and public interest.

Oversight is not distrust of intelligence services; it is the condition that allows a democracy to trust them at all. Secret power cannot be made fully visible without destroying its usefulness, but it cannot be left to justify itself in darkness. Democratic oversight exists in that difficult middle ground.

Traditional oversight was designed for a world in which surveillance was costly, targeted, and relatively visible. In that world, parliaments, courts, and review bodies could focus on authorisations for specific operations and on ex post reports about defined programs. Mass digital collection and secret legal interpretations break this frame. They allow whole categories of activity to be normalised in classified annexes, technical protocols, and closed-door agreements that most citizens, and many legislators, never see. If oversight accepts this logic and limits itself to verifying internal compliance with secret rules, it risks becoming a management tool for the security bureaucracy rather than an instrument of democratic control. The basic question, then, is no longer only whether services obey the law, but who writes that law, who can contest it, and at what point secrecy about surveillance becomes incompatible with the idea of government by the consent of the governed.

When Secret Law Eats Public Law: Mass Surveillance and Hidden Interpretations

Debates about mass surveillance in the early twenty-first century revealed not only the scale of technical collection, but also the existence of what critics call "secret law." In many democratic states, constitutions and public statutes formally guaranteed strong protections for privacy, freedom of expression, and the confidentiality of communications. On paper, intrusive surveillance was permitted only under clear legal conditions, subject to judicial authorisation and proportionality tests. Yet disclosures by whistleblowers and subsequent court cases showed that security and intelligence services were operating under classified legal interpretations that effectively widened their powers far beyond what the public texts appeared to allow.

In such systems, framework laws may look restrictive, while executive branches, agencies, or specialized courts develop secret interpretations that redefine key concepts: “relevance,” “foreign intelligence,” “metadata,” or “national security.” The public reads one legal order; the agencies operate under another.

“Secret law” captures this gap between formal rights and operational practice. Rights remain on paper, but confidential interpretations can turn exceptional measures into routine tools while keeping the reasoning out of public view.

Secret Services Against Social Movements and Resistance

Secret services are usually described as institutions designed to protect societies from danger: espionage, terrorism, sabotage, foreign interference, organized violence, and threats to constitutional order. In official language, their purpose is defensive. They guard the state, protect citizens, and help governments understand hidden risks. Yet the historical record shows a more troubling pattern. Intelligence agencies have often defined "security" in ways that protect not only people from violence, but also ruling classes, racial hierarchies, colonial relationships, corporate interests, geopolitical spheres of influence, and existing forms of social order.

This does not mean that every intelligence operation is reducible to repression or domination. States do face real threats, and some intelligence work has prevented violence, exposed espionage, and helped decision-makers avoid catastrophe. But the central question is not only whether secret services protect security, but whose security they protect, whose freedom they limit, and which social arrangements they help preserve.

Again and again, movements seeking racial equality, labor rights, land reform, decolonization, socialist transformation, national sovereignty, anti-war politics, environmental protection, or democratic accountability have been treated as security problems. Sometimes this involved surveillance. Sometimes infiltration. Sometimes propaganda, disruption, blacklisting, cooperation with employers, or covert support for opposition forces. In more extreme cases, intelligence and security networks became entangled with coups, counterinsurgency, torture, disappearances, and mass political violence.

The pattern is not limited to authoritarian regimes. It appears in liberal democracies, colonial systems, military dictatorships, apartheid states, Cold War client regimes, and contemporary digital surveillance systems. What changes is the vocabulary. One period speaks of "subversion" and "communist infiltration." Another speaks of "extremism," "public order," "counterterrorism," "stability," "critical infrastructure," or "hybrid threats." But beneath these terms lies a recurring political logic: when organized groups challenge dominant power, intelligence agencies may treat emancipation itself as a danger.

Race: surveillance of liberation movements

One of the clearest examples is the use of domestic intelligence against racial justice and Black liberation movements. In the United States, the FBI's COINTELPRO operations targeted civil rights activists, Black radical organizations, anti-war groups, Indigenous activists, socialist organizations, and other political movements. The targets were not simply foreign agents or armed conspiracies. They included people and organizations demanding racial equality, economic justice, and an end to state violence.

The significance of COINTELPRO is not only that the FBI exceeded legal or ethical limits. Its deeper importance lies in what it reveals about the political definition of threat. Black liberation, anti-racist organizing, and radical democratic demands were not treated merely as legitimate political expression; they were often interpreted as forms of disorder, subversion, or danger to the state. The language of national security became a way to police movements that challenged racial hierarchy and the legitimacy of existing institutions.

This pattern shows how intelligence agencies can become guardians of racial order. They do not need to openly defend racism in ideological language. It is enough to frame anti-racist mobilization as instability, radicalization, extremism, or a threat to public order. Once that framing is accepted, surveillance and disruption can appear as neutral security work rather than political repression.

Class: labor movements, unions, and economic order

Intelligence agencies have also monitored labor movements, unions, miners, industrial workers, and socialist or communist organizations. In capitalist democracies, labor conflict has often been treated not only as an economic dispute, but as a potential threat to national stability. Strikes, workplace militancy, and radical union activity could be reframed as subversion, foreign influence, or danger to public order.

This is crucial for a left-critical reading of intelligence power. When workers organize for better wages, safer conditions, public ownership, workplace democracy, or broader social redistribution, they challenge not only individual employers but the structure of economic power. Intelligence agencies may then act, directly or indirectly, to protect "stability" – but stability can mean the stability of existing property relations, corporate authority, and class hierarchy.

In Britain, controversies around the monitoring of trade unionists and miners' strikes illustrate this problem. In the United States, labor organizers were frequently watched through anti-communist frameworks. In many countries, intelligence files on union activists blurred the line between security concerns and class control. The state did not always need to break strikes openly. It could gather information, identify leaders, share concerns with employers, infiltrate organizations, or classify radical labor politics as a security risk.

The deeper point is that "economic stability" is never politically neutral. For workers, instability may mean unemployment, poverty, exploitation, or unsafe work. For employers and governments, instability may mean strikes, disruption of production, or threats to investment. Intelligence agencies often operate from the perspective of the state and dominant institutions, which means they are structurally inclined to treat challenges from below as risks to be managed.

Empire: coups, covert action, and anti-communist intervention

The Cold War made this logic global. Across Latin America, Africa, Asia, and the Middle East, intelligence services – especially those of major powers – participated in covert operations against governments and movements that challenged Western geopolitical and economic interests. These interventions were usually justified through anti-communism. But the targets were often broader than Soviet-aligned forces. They included nationalist, reformist, socialist, non-aligned, anti-colonial, and redistributive projects.

Guatemala, Iran, Chile, Nicaragua, Congo, Indonesia, El Salvador, and other cases reveal a recurring pattern. Governments that attempted land reform, nationalization of resources, redistribution of wealth, or independent foreign policy were framed as strategic threats. Intelligence agencies did not simply observe these developments; in several cases, they helped destabilize governments, fund opposition groups, support military actors, conduct propaganda, or assist counterinsurgency forces.

In Guatemala, land reform threatened the interests of United Fruit and local elites. In Iran, oil nationalization threatened British and Western control over a strategic resource. In Chile, Salvador Allende's democratic socialist project challenged both domestic elites and American corporate and geopolitical interests. In Nicaragua, the Sandinista revolution represented the possibility of an alternative political model in Central America. In Congo, Patrice Lumumba's postcolonial nationalism and insistence on sovereignty over resources made him suspect within Cold War calculations.

What links these cases is not that they were identical. Each had local conflicts, internal divisions, and specific historical conditions. The common thread is that intelligence agencies often interpreted social transformation as geopolitical danger. Anti-communism became a flexible language through which land reform, national independence, labor mobilization, resource sovereignty, and socialist politics could be treated as threats to security.

Counterinsurgency: when social reform becomes an enemy

In many countries, intelligence services did not act alone. They worked through military, police, paramilitary, and client-state structures. This is especially visible in Central America, where counterinsurgency blurred the line between intelligence work and political terror. Security forces targeted guerrillas, but also peasants, unionists, priests, students, teachers, journalists, and community organizers accused of sympathizing with the left.

The political meaning of counterinsurgency is broader than military conflict. It is a method of governing society under conditions of perceived internal threat. Intelligence identifies networks, maps communities, classifies populations, distinguishes loyal citizens from suspect ones, and helps security forces decide who should be watched, intimidated, recruited, displaced, detained, or eliminated. In such contexts, the "enemy" is often not only an armed group, but the social base of reform itself.

This is why counterinsurgency is so important for a left-critical analysis of secret services. It shows intelligence not as passive information-gathering, but as part of a machinery for preventing social transformation. When poverty, land inequality, racial exclusion, and class conflict produce resistance, intelligence systems may translate those struggles into the language of subversion. The solution then becomes not justice or redistribution, but surveillance, infiltration, pacification, and repression.

Apartheid: intelligence in defense of racial capitalism

Apartheid South Africa offers another powerful example. The apartheid state used intelligence and security services to monitor and suppress liberation movements, anti-apartheid activists, trade unions, student organizations, exiles, and international solidarity networks. These services were not merely defending the state against violence. They were defending a racial and economic order built on dispossession, segregation, cheap Black labor, and political exclusion.

This case is especially important because it makes visible what is sometimes hidden in other contexts: security can be the name a regime gives to the preservation of domination. Apartheid intelligence agencies treated the demand for equality as a threat because equality would have destroyed the political and economic foundations of the regime. The "security" of apartheid meant the insecurity of the oppressed majority.

The same logic appears elsewhere, though often in less explicit forms. When intelligence agencies protect a social order based on racial hierarchy, colonial extraction, or economic exploitation, they do not merely protect institutions. They protect the unequal distribution of life chances.

Anti-colonial movements and postcolonial sovereignty

Secret services have also played major roles in colonial and postcolonial contexts. Colonial administrations relied on intelligence to monitor nationalist movements, labor unrest, anti-colonial parties, student groups, newspapers, and religious or cultural organizations. Intelligence was a tool of empire because empire depended on knowing, classifying, and controlling subject populations.

After formal decolonization, the logic often continued in new forms. Postcolonial leaders who pursued non-alignment, nationalization, resource sovereignty, or socialist development were frequently viewed with suspicion by former colonial powers and Cold War blocs. Intelligence cooperation, covert influence, elite networks, military assistance, and economic pressure could all be used to keep newly independent states within acceptable limits.

This is where cases such as Congo, Françafrique[1], and other postcolonial intelligence networks become important. They show that empire did not disappear simply because formal colonial rule ended. It often survived through security partnerships, military advisers, covert influence, resource politics, and intelligence ties with local elites. The question was no longer always direct colonial command, but the management of sovereignty: how independent could a newly independent country actually be?

Social movements: environmentalists, anti-globalization activists, and civil society

In more recent decades, intelligence and security agencies have monitored environmental activists, anti-globalization movements, anti-war groups, racial justice movements, migrant solidarity networks, and other civil society actors. Some of these movements included fringe elements willing to break laws or engage in property damage. But many targets were overwhelmingly peaceful political actors.

The issue is not whether states may investigate specific crimes. The issue is the expansion of the security frame to whole movements. Environmental protest can be treated as a threat to energy infrastructure. Anti-globalization activism can be treated as disorder. Migrant solidarity can be associated with border security. Anti-war organizing can be framed as foreign-influenced. The more elastic the concept of security becomes, the easier it is to place dissent under suspicion.

This is especially dangerous because social movements are often the means by which democratic societies correct injustice. Many rights now considered normal were won by movements once described as radical, disruptive, dangerous, or subversive. If intelligence agencies treat such movements primarily as threats, they help freeze the existing order and narrow the field of democratic possibility.

War on Terror: racialized suspicion and preventive surveillance

After 11 September 2001, the War on Terror produced a vast expansion of surveillance, watchlisting, intelligence-sharing, border control, and preventive policing. Muslim, Arab, South Asian, migrant, and refugee communities were often placed under heightened suspicion. Mosques, charities, student groups, travel patterns, online activity, and community networks became objects of intelligence interest.

This was not only a response to terrorism. It also created a racialized security order in which entire populations were treated as reservoirs of potential threat. In practice, this means that suspicion is not distributed evenly across society; it attaches more easily to certain names, bodies, languages, neighborhoods, travel routes, and religious institutions. The burden of suspicion was unevenly distributed. Some citizens moved through society as presumptively innocent; others were more likely to be watched, questioned, profiled, or classified as risky.

This shows how intelligence power intersects with race, migration, empire, and war. Foreign military interventions and domestic surveillance became part of the same security architecture. The external enemy and the internal suspect were connected through a global language of counterterrorism.

Digital surveillance: from state files to data infrastructures

The digital era has transformed the scale and texture of intelligence power. Earlier intelligence systems relied on informers, wiretaps, files, intercepted mail, physical surveillance, and human networks. Contemporary systems can draw on communications metadata, social media, commercial databases, biometric systems, location data, financial records, predictive analytics, and platform infrastructures.

The Snowden revelations exposed the extent to which modern intelligence agencies could operate through global communications networks and private technology companies. Programs such as PRISM[2] raised fundamental questions about the relationship between state surveillance and corporate data collection. The issue was no longer simply that governments watched citizens. It was that the everyday architecture of digital life had become usable for intelligence purposes.

This creates a new form of asymmetry. Citizens produce data as they communicate, shop, move, work, search, travel, and socialize. Corporations extract value from this data. States can then access, request, purchase, intercept, or analyze parts of it. The individual becomes simultaneously a citizen, consumer, data source, and potential intelligence object.

Privatized intelligence: Pegasus, spyware, and the market for repression

The rise of commercial spyware adds another layer. Tools such as Pegasus[3] show how capabilities once associated with advanced state intelligence agencies can be developed by private firms and sold to governments. These tools can be used against serious security threats, but investigations have shown their use against journalists, opposition figures, human rights defenders, lawyers, activists, and civil society actors.

This is one of the clearest contemporary examples of the privatization of intelligence power. Repression becomes a market. Surveillance becomes a commodity. Governments no longer need to build every capability internally; they can buy access to tools, expertise, and infrastructure from private vendors. The result is a global security industry that can strengthen authoritarian practices even in states that lack advanced domestic intelligence capacities.

---

2. PRISM was one of the surveillance programs revealed by Edward Snowden in 2013, involving access to data from major technology companies under U.S. legal authorities. "Upstream collection" refers to the interception of communications as they move through internet backbone infrastructure, rather than only from individual company accounts or devices.

3. Pegasus is spyware developed by the Israeli company NSO Group. It has been reported to infect smartphones and enable access to messages, calls, microphones, cameras, and location data, and has been linked by investigators and rights organizations to surveillance of journalists, activists, lawyers, politicians, and dissidents in several countries.

The issue here is not only privacy. It is political economy. Who profits from surveillance? Who sells the tools of repression? Which states buy them? Which populations become testing grounds? Which activists, journalists, and opposition groups pay the price? Intelligence power is no longer only a state secret; it is also a business model.

A recurring pattern

Across these examples – COINTELPRO, labor surveillance, anti-communist covert action, counterinsurgency, apartheid, postcolonial intervention, War on Terror surveillance, NSA programs, and commercial spyware – one pattern becomes visible: intelligence agencies often operate at the boundary between security and social control.

They define threats. They classify populations. They produce knowledge for power. They decide which movements deserve attention, which actors are suspicious, which forms of dissent are tolerable, and which demands appear dangerous. Their work may be justified as protecting the public, but it can also protect property, empire, racial order, class power, and geopolitical hierarchy.

This is why secret services must be analyzed not only as technical institutions, but as political institutions. The key question is not simply whether they obey procedures, whether they are efficient, or whether they are overseen by formal bodies. The deeper question is what kind of society their work helps reproduce.

When intelligence is used against emancipatory movements, it does not only gather information. It shapes history by narrowing the possibilities of liberation. It makes some futures easier to imagine and others easier to destroy. It protects the present against those who try to transform it.

That is the central lesson of intelligence against emancipation: secret services do not merely defend states from threats. In many historical moments, they have defended existing orders from freedom movements that asked whether those states, economies, and empires had the right to exist in their current form.

Intelligence in Authoritarian and Transitional Regimes

In an authoritarian state, the knock on the door does not always come at night. Sometimes it comes as a warning from an employer, a cancelled promotion, a file quietly opened, a friend who suddenly asks too many questions, or a rumor that one's name has appeared in the records of the service. Fear does not need to be spectacular to be effective. It works best when it becomes part of ordinary calculation: what can be said, who can be trusted, which meeting is safe, which joke should remain unspoken.

This is where secret services become something more than instruments of national security. They become managers of silence. Their task is no longer only to discover spies, terrorists, or foreign threats, but to define the boundaries of permitted life. A citizen may never see the archive, never meet the officer, never know who reported them. Yet the possibility of being watched can shape behavior as powerfully as direct repression.

When such regimes collapse, the secret service does not simply disappear with the old flag, party, or leader. Its files remain. Its officers may find new uniforms. Its informers may enter business, politics, media, or the police. Its habits of secrecy may survive inside institutions that now speak the language of democracy. The most difficult question is therefore not only how secret services serve authoritarian power, but how their shadows continue to shape societies after authoritarianism formally ends.

Repression, Fear, and the Legacy of Secret Police

When intelligence and security services operate inside authoritarian and totalitarian systems, their logic changes. Instead of being primarily instruments for understanding and managing external threats, they become central tools for controlling society from within. Their core mission is not to protect a constitutional order shared by citizens, but to protect a ruling group, party, or ideology against real and imagined enemies. To understand the darker side of secret services, it is necessary to examine how they function in such regimes–and what happens when those regimes collapse or formally democratize.

Structural Features of Authoritarian and Totalitarian Services

Authoritarian and totalitarian secret services share several structural traits that distinguish them from their counterparts in democracies, even when they use similar technologies and organizational forms.

Dense networks of informers

A hallmark of many repressive systems is the creation of extensive networks of informers embedded in workplaces, neighborhoods, universities, religious communities, and families. Ordinary citizens are pressured or incentivized to report on each other's conversations, activities, and attitudes. The goal is not only to detect plots but to make people uncertain about whom to trust. This uncertainty encourages self-censorship and discourages collective action.

Political police at the core

In these regimes, the boundary between intelligence, security, and political police disappears. Agencies are tasked explicitly with monitoring and suppressing political opposition, ideological deviation, and independent organization. Files are kept on dissidents, critical intellectuals, artists, union organizers, and sometimes entire demographic groups. Security organs may be directly involved in managing party structures, vetting officials, and guiding appointments.

Ideological control

Totalitarian systems, in particular, use secret services to enforce ideological conformity. Surveillance and repression target not only overt acts but also suspected attitudes. Reading forbidden books, telling jokes, or voicing doubts can attract attention. Security organs work closely with propaganda and censorship offices to silence alternative narratives. The aim is to create an environment in which the regime's version of reality is the only one that can be safely expressed.

Violence and coercion

Repressive services possess broad powers to detain, interrogate, and punish. Methods range from harassment and job loss to imprisonment, torture, and extrajudicial killing. Violence serves both an instrumental and a symbolic purpose: it neutralizes specific individuals and sends a message to others about the costs of disobedience. Legal procedures, where they exist, are often formalities, with outcomes determined in advance by security organs.

Institutional depth and redundancy

Authoritarian regimes often create multiple overlapping security agencies, each monitoring different sectors and sometimes each other. This redundancy is meant to prevent any single organization from becoming powerful enough to threaten the leadership, while ensuring that no segment of society escapes surveillance. Ministries of interior, national security committees, military intelligence, party control commissions, and secret police units all form parts of a dense web.

Together, these features produce a system in which fear and uncertainty become tools of governance. Citizens learn that certain topics are dangerous, that private spaces may not be safe, and that the state has long memory and wide reach.

Serving the Regime, Not the State

The crucial difference between intelligence in authoritarian regimes and in democracies is their ultimate reference point. In authoritarian and totalitarian systems, secret services serve the regime–its leadership, its party, its ideological project–not the state as a community of citizens.

This shows up in several ways:

Definition of threats: A threat is not defined primarily by the risk of violence or external aggression, but by the risk of political challenge. Peaceful opposition, independent media, and civil society organization are treated as hostile acts because they might undermine the regime's grip on power.

Targets of surveillance: Instead of focusing on individuals plotting terrorism, espionage, or sabotage, services focus on those with influence: intellectuals, community leaders, religious figures, activists, opposition politicians, and even members of the elite who seem insufficiently loyal.

Use of information: Intelligence about people's personal lives–affairs, debts, addictions, family problems–is used for blackmail, recruitment, and control, not for protecting public safety. Files become tools for managing elites and ordinary citizens alike.

Absence of independent oversight: Courts, parliaments, and media are subordinated or controlled. Oversight bodies, if they exist, are part of the same power structure and do not challenge the services. Secrecy protects the regime from the people, not the people from external threats.

In such systems, secret services are central pillars of power. They help prevent coups, manage intra-elite conflicts, and suppress grassroots movements. Even when they perform some traditional intelligence functions–such as monitoring foreign rivals–their defining role is domestic control.

Transition: What Happens When Regimes Change?

When authoritarian regimes collapse or attempt to transition toward democracy, the fate of their secret services becomes a critical question. These organizations embody the old order's methods and secrets. How they are handled can profoundly affect the trajectory of the new system.

Lustration and vetting

One approach is lustration: screening individuals who worked in repressive security organs and barring some of them from holding public office or sensitive positions. The aim is to prevent those who committed serious abuses from returning to positions of power and to signal a moral break with the past. Lustration policies vary widely in scope, fairness, and effectiveness. Too broad, and they risk turning into collective punishment or paralyzing institutions; too narrow, and they fail to address public anger and mistrust.

Reform and restructuring

New governments may choose to dissolve old agencies, create new ones, or radically reform existing structures. This can involve rewriting legal mandates, changing leadership, establishing new oversight mechanisms, and retraining personnel. The challenge is to build security services that can handle real threats–organized crime, extremism, foreign interference–without reproducing the logic of political policing. In practice, reforms are often partial and contested.

Continuity of personnel

In many transitions, the majority of staff from old services remain in place, at least initially. Their skills and institutional knowledge are difficult to replace overnight. This continuity can have advantages for technical capacity but also carries risks: old networks, attitudes, and loyalties may persist beneath new legal frameworks. Informal hierarchies and habits of secrecy can survive regime change.

Selective opening of archives

Another key issue is what to do with the archives of secret police and intelligence services. Opening archives can serve truth, justice, and historical understanding. It can allow victims to see what was recorded about them, expose past abuses, and document the mechanics of repression. However, opening archives can also destabilize by revealing collaboration, provoking personal and political conflicts, and giving rise to selective use of files for new political battles.

Some states have established independent archives authorities to manage access, protect privacy where necessary, and prevent manipulation. Others have kept archives largely closed, citing security or stability. Selective leaks and partial openings, controlled by political actors, can turn the legacy of secret services into a weapon in contemporary struggles.

Long-Term Effects: Fear, Trust, and Conspiracy

Even after formal structures are reformed, the legacy of authoritarian secret services lingers in social attitudes and political culture.

Culture of fear and self-censorship

People who lived under intensive surveillance may continue to censor themselves long after legal risks diminish. Memories of past repression shape how they assess current threats. They may be wary of engaging in politics, joining organizations, or expressing dissenting views. This can weaken democratic participation and civil society.

Distrust of institutions

Where secret services were pervasive and abusive, trust in state institutions often remains low. Citizens may assume that new agencies are simply rebranded versions of old ones, no matter what laws say. They may suspect that judges, police, and politicians are still entangled with hidden networks. This distrust can fuel disengagement from formal politics and strengthen the appeal of populist or anti-system narratives.

Conspiracy thinking

A history of genuine conspiracies–secret operations, informers, politically motivated prosecutions–creates fertile ground for broader conspiracy theories. People who know that the state once lied systematically find it harder to believe official explanations even when they are honest. Events are easily interpreted as the work of hidden services, and rumors can spread quickly. This can distort public debate and make it harder to build consensus around reforms.

Instrumentalization of the past

The legacy of secret services can itself be politicized. Parties and leaders may use accusations of collaboration, selective archive revelations, or ambiguous references to "files" as tools to discredit opponents. Instead of fostering a shared understanding of past abuses, the history of repression becomes a battlefield for present power struggles. This perpetuates division and prevents closure.

Understanding the Logic of Repressive Models and Their Successors

For a global reader, emblematic cases like the Nazi Gestapo, the Soviet KGB, the East German Stasi, or Yugoslav and other Eastern European secret police services illustrate the extreme forms of repressive intelligence systems. These organizations combined ideological zeal, bureaucratic methods, and a readiness to use violence. They monitored society in depth, targeted perceived enemies, and maintained regimes that presented themselves as unshakable.

Yet even these services had weaknesses. They were plagued by internal rivalries, corruption, misperceptions, and overreach. Their reliance on fear and secrecy undermined genuine social trust and innovation. When regimes weakened–through economic crisis, external pressure, or internal dissent–the same structures that had once enforced stability contributed to brittle collapse.

In transitional societies, the successors to these services operate in a more ambiguous environment. They may formally serve democratic institutions, but they inherit personnel, habits, and sometimes archives from their predecessors. Political elites may still be tempted to use them for partisan purposes. Citizens may still assume that "nothing has really changed."

Building democratic intelligence services is not a matter of changing names or passing new laws. It requires reshaping mandates, organizational cultures, oversight, archives, and public debate.

Secret services in authoritarian and transitional regimes show, in a concentrated form, the dangers inherent in secret power. They demonstrate how easily the logic of security can be twisted into the logic of control, how fear can become a governing tool, and how long the shadows of secrecy can stretch into the future. Understanding their history and legacy is not only a matter of condemning past abuses. It is a warning about what can happen whenever secret institutions are freed from law, accountability, and genuine public purpose.

The legacy of secret police survives in archives, careers, habits, fears, informal loyalties, and public suspicion. New elections and constitutions may change the surface of political life, but they do not automatically transform institutions once built around files, informers, and invisible influence. That inheritance must be confronted rather than hidden.

Old Regime, New Uniforms: Reforming Services in Post-Communist Europe

After 1989, the new democratic governments in Central and Eastern Europe faced a central dilemma: what to do with the security and intelligence services inherited from communist regimes. The Czechoslovak – and later Czech – approach offers an illustrative example. The communist State Security (StB) had combined political policing with extensive domestic surveillance and cooperation with foreign intelligence, leaving behind not only repressive practices but also voluminous archives and dense informal networks. The fear was that, if left intact, these structures and personnel could quietly undermine democratic institutions from within.

Czechoslovakia adopted one of the region's most far-reaching lustration laws in 1991. It barred former high-ranking communist officials, StB officers, and registered collaborators from many public positions, including in the judiciary, prosecution, senior civil service, security sector, state enterprises, and public media.

The model was controversial. Supporters saw lustration as necessary to protect fragile democracy and mark a break with repression. Critics warned of injustice, collective stigma, politicized files, and guilt by association. The case shows that confronting a secret-police legacy requires both moral clarity and procedural restraint.

Yugoslav and Post-Yugoslav Experiences of Political Policing

The Yugoslav State Security Service, known first as UDBA and later as SDB, combined intelligence and political-police functions throughout socialist Yugoslavia. Formally tasked with protecting the state from "internal and external enemies," it monitored émigrés, nationalists, dissidents, religious communities, and ideological opponents, while also conducting foreign intelligence and counterintelligence work.

In the late socialist period, especially after the 1960s, formal political repression became somewhat less overt, but the security apparatus remained central to managing ideological conformity and suppressing challenges to the federal order. With the disintegration of Yugoslavia, republican branches of the service were transformed into new state security bodies under emerging post-Yugoslav governments, often with significant continuity of personnel, methods, and informal networks. In several successor states, state security structures played controversial roles during the wars of the 1990s, in political violence, and in the protection or facilitation of organized crime, further blurring the line between "security service," political police, and patronage network.

The post-Yugoslav period remains marked by unresolved archives and informal power. Most regional states moved slowly on opening files or adopting robust lustration frameworks, leaving debates about collaboration, legitimacy, and continuity politically explosive. This uneven reckoning has allowed suspicions about old networks to persist in public life.

The Digital Turn

The old spy followed a person through a street, opened a letter, recruited a source, or listened through a wall. The new intelligence world often begins somewhere less visible: inside a phone carried in a pocket, a search typed late at night, a message stored on a server, a location ping sent by an app, or a pattern detected in millions of ordinary digital traces. The target may never see the observer. The observer may not even be a state agency at first, but a company, a platform, a data broker, or an algorithm sorting behavior into categories of interest.

This is the quiet revolution that has transformed secret power. Surveillance no longer depends only on agents, informers, microphones, or intercepted radio signals. Modern life produces data continuously, and that data can be collected, bought, combined, stored, searched, and interpreted long after the moment has passed. A person's movements, contacts, habits, fears, purchases, beliefs, and associations can become visible not through one dramatic act of spying, but through the ordinary infrastructure of digital life.

The digital turn therefore changes more than the tools of intelligence. It changes the relationship between citizen, state, and corporation. Secret services gain new ways to know, predict, and influence. Private companies become holders of information once available only to governments. Citizens become both users of technology and sources of data. The central question is no longer only whether someone is being watched, but who is doing the watching, who owns the traces, who interprets them, and what happens when the machinery of security joins with the machinery of the market.

Cyber Intelligence, Mass Surveillance, and Data-Driven Power

The digital revolution has transformed almost every aspect of modern life–and secret services are no exception. Where earlier generations of intelligence relied on letters, radio signals, physical surveillance, and human sources, contemporary services operate in a world where communications, commerce, politics, and private life all leave dense digital traces. This creates unprecedented opportunities for intelligence agencies, but also unprecedented risks for privacy, freedom, and the balance of power between citizens, states, and corporations.

To understand this new landscape, it is useful to distinguish several interconnected developments: cyber espionage, mass surveillance, the role of private data industries, the rise of artificial intelligence and predictive analytics, and the emergence of hybrid operations that blend intelligence with information warfare.

Cyber Espionage: Intrusions, Data Theft, and Persistent Operations

Cyber espionage refers to the use of digital means–network intrusions, malware, phishing, and other techniques–to penetrate computer systems and steal information. It is an extension of traditional spying into the digital realm, but with distinct characteristics.

Network intrusions and APT campaigns

Advanced Persistent Threat (APT)[1] operations involve stealthy, long-term penetration of networks. Attackers may gain access through phishing emails, exploiting software vulnerabilities, or compromising supply chains. Once inside, they move laterally, escalate privileges, and establish backdoors to maintain access

1. Advanced Persistent Threat (APT) is a cybersecurity term for a sustained, stealthy, and often state-linked intrusion campaign in which attackers maintain long-term access to a target network. Unlike simple one-off attacks, APT operations are usually designed for continuous intelligence collection, strategic positioning, or preparation for later disruption.

over time. The goal is not quick disruption but ongoing collection of sensitive information: diplomatic cables, defense plans, research data, corporate secrets.

Industrial and political espionage

Cyber operations target not only military and intelligence systems but also universities, tech companies, critical infrastructure operators, and political organizations. Industrial espionage seeks to acquire trade secrets, technological designs, and strategic business information that can benefit domestic industries or state-owned enterprises. Political espionage focuses on party communications, campaign strategies, and internal government deliberations, providing insight into how other states think and plan.

Attraction of cyber espionage

For states, cyber espionage offers several advantages. It can be relatively cheap compared to traditional HUMINT operations, scalable across many targets, and conducted at long range. It can be difficult to attribute with certainty, allowing plausible deniability. It can also blur the line between intelligence collection and preparation for potential sabotage, as access gained for spying can later be used to disrupt systems if tensions escalate.

As more of the world's sensitive information resides on interconnected networks, the incentives for cyber espionage grow. At the same time, the difficulty of securing complex systems means that even well-resourced organizations struggle to keep determined state-linked actors out.

Mass Surveillance: Bulk Collection, Metadata, and the Dream of Total Awareness

Traditional surveillance focused on specific targets: particular phones, addresses, or individuals. Digital technologies have enabled a shift toward mass surveillance, in which vast quantities of data are collected, stored, and analyzed in bulk.

Bulk collection and metadata

Instead of intercepting only the content of selected communications, some programs collect large datasets–phone records, internet traffic, location data–from entire populations or broad categories of users. Metadata (who communicated with whom, when, from where, using what device) can reveal social networks, movement patterns, and habits even without accessing content. The logic is that collecting everything now may allow useful analysis later.

Algorithmic filtering and retention

Because humans cannot manually review such volumes, agencies rely on automated systems to filter and flag data. Algorithms search for patterns associated with known threats, generate risk scores, and select items for closer scrutiny. Retention policies determine how long data is kept; in some systems, records are stored for years, allowing retrospective analysis if someone later becomes a person of interest.

The "total information awareness" mindset

Mass surveillance can encourage a mentality in which more data is always better, where the ideal is to miss nothing. The hope is that by monitoring as much as possible, agencies can detect weak signals of emerging threats, connect disparate clues, and prevent attacks. But this mindset underestimates the problems of noise, false positives, and the chilling effects of pervasive monitoring. It also shifts the default assumption about privacy: instead of being left alone unless there is reason to suspect wrongdoing, individuals may be monitored by default, with protections relying on internal rules rather than external limits.

Risks and controversies

Mass surveillance raises profound legal and ethical questions. Bulk collection often stretches or reinterprets existing laws designed for targeted interception. It can disproportionately affect minorities, activists, journalists, and political opponents if filters or watchlists reflect biased assumptions. The mere knowledge that communications may be stored and analyzed can discourage free expression and association, altering the fabric of democratic life.

Private Power: Companies, Platforms, and Data Brokers

The digital intelligence landscape is not shaped by states alone. Private companies play a central role in creating, collecting, and analyzing data.

Telecoms, platforms, and cloud providers

Telecommunications companies, internet service providers, and cloud platforms carry and store vast amounts of data. Social media companies host intimate details of users' lives: social networks, interests, locations, and opinions. These companies may be legally compelled to cooperate with intelligence and law-enforcement requests, or they may voluntarily share certain data. Their technical architectures–encryption practices, logging policies, data localization–profoundly influence what states can access.

Data brokers and commercial surveillance

A global industry of data brokers[2] collects, aggregates, and sells personal data: location histories, purchase habits, health indicators, browsing patterns, and more. This data is often derived from apps, loyalty programs, online tracking, and public records. Intelligence and security agencies can purchase or otherwise access such data, sometimes circumventing stricter legal standards that apply to direct surveillance. The boundary between commercial profiling and state surveillance becomes porous.

Private intelligence and cyber firms

Security companies, consultants, and private intelligence firms develop tools for intrusion, surveillance, and analysis. Some sell exploits and spyware to govern-

2. Data brokers are companies that collect, aggregate, analyze, and sell personal or organizational data, often derived from apps, online tracking, purchases, location services, public records, and advertising systems. Their databases can become useful to governments and security agencies because they contain information that would once have required direct surveillance or legal authorization to obtain.

ments, including regimes with weak human-rights protections. Others provide defensive services, incident response, and threat intelligence. The commercialization of capabilities once confined to state agencies changes the ecology of power: more actors have access to sophisticated tools, but regulatory frameworks lag behind.

The involvement of private actors complicates accountability. Citizens often do not know how their data is collected, where it goes, or how it might be used by states. Oversight mechanisms designed for public institutions may not fully reach into private data markets, even when those markets effectively supply the raw material for intelligence.

The result is a three-way asymmetry of power: states command coercion and institutional authority, corporations control infrastructure and data, while citizens simultaneously lose sight of who is tracking them, on what basis, and for which purposes. In such an order, the classic opposition of "state versus citizen" is no longer sufficient: surveillance becomes a joint product of state and private actors, while the individual is the one who knows the least and decides the least.

AI, Big Data, and Predictive Analytics in Intelligence

As data volumes grow, intelligence agencies increasingly turn to artificial intelligence (AI) and machine learning to make sense of them. These technologies promise to detect patterns that humans might miss, automate routine analysis, and support predictive assessments.

Pattern recognition and anomaly detection

Machine learning systems can be trained to recognize patterns associated with certain risks: unusual travel patterns, bursts of communications in specific networks, financial transactions that match known laundering schemes, or online behavior linked to extremist recruitment. They can flag anomalies–behaviors that deviate from norms–for further investigation.

Automated triage and prioritization

AI tools can help prioritize leads, rank targets, and allocate human analytic resources. By scoring large numbers of data points, they can direct human attention to cases deemed most urgent or most likely to involve serious threats. This can improve efficiency in theory, though it also risks embedding existing biases into automated systems.

Predictive analytics

Some projects aim to go beyond detection to prediction: estimating who might become involved in crime or terrorism, which regions are at risk of unrest, or how likely certain scenarios are to unfold. These efforts blend historical data, behavioral models, and machine learning to produce forecasts. While alluring, such systems often rely on assumptions that are hard to validate and can produce self-fulfilling or discriminatory outcomes if used to justify preemptive measures.

Risks and limitations

AI systems are not neutral. They reflect the data they are trained on, the objectives they are given, and the choices of their designers. If training data encodes historical biases–e.g., disproportionate policing of certain communities–then predictive tools may reinforce those patterns, directing more scrutiny to already over-policed groups. Opaque models can make it difficult to understand why certain individuals or behaviors are flagged, complicating legal challenge and accountability.

Moreover, AI can create a false sense of certainty. Outputs may be treated as objective truths rather than probabilistic estimates. Decision-makers may become over-reliant on algorithmic rankings, especially when under pressure. The combination of secrecy, complexity, and high stakes makes it difficult to scrutinize or contest automated intelligence judgments.

When systems whose workings cannot easily be explained draw the line between what is "normal" and what is "suspicious," the deepest political decisions enter this algorithmic space of silencing and selection – but without open political debate. In effect, a part of sovereignty is shifted from visible institutions into the invisible architecture of code.

Hybrid Operations: Disinformation and Psychological Campaigns

Digital technologies have also expanded the field of information operations, where intelligence, propaganda, and psychological tactics converge. Secret services and related actors use online platforms not only to collect information but to shape perceptions.

Disinformation campaigns

States and aligned groups deploy networks of fake accounts, bots, and controlled media outlets to spread misleading or false narratives. These campaigns may aim to influence elections, exacerbate social divisions, undermine trust in institutions, or discredit opponents. They often combine genuine grievances with fabricated content, making them harder to counter.

Psychological operations on social media

Data about users' preferences, fears, and networks can be used to micro-target messages. Tailored content can exploit existing biases, reinforce echo chambers, and manipulate emotions. In some cases, intelligence agencies or their partners design content that appears organic–memes, videos, "grassroots" pages–while masking its origin.

Blurring of foreign and domestic

Hybrid operations challenge traditional distinctions between foreign and domestic intelligence. A campaign launched by a foreign service may target domestic audiences through local proxies. Domestic actors may amplify foreign narratives that suit their interests. Secret services may be involved in defending against such campaigns, but in some systems they may also be involved in conducting them, raising serious questions about manipulation of their own populations.

Attribution and response

Attributing disinformation and influence operations to specific actors is technically and politically difficult. Plausible deniability is built into the use of cut-outs, front organizations, and anonymous accounts. Responses–ranging from platform moderation and counter-messaging to sanctions and public exposure–require coordination between governments, companies, and civil society. Intelligence agencies may contribute by identifying networks and methods, but their involvement in public communication raises sensitive issues about domestic influence.

Technology, Power, and Freedom

The digital turn has undeniably increased the capabilities of secret services. Cyber espionage opens doors into systems and conversations that were once inaccessible. Mass surveillance and data aggregation allow unprecedented mapping of societies. AI and analytics offer new ways of extracting insight from noise. Information operations provide new instruments of influence short of war.

These developments also intensify the risks to freedom. When surveillance is pervasive and largely invisible, the traditional safeguards of liberal societies–warrants, individualized suspicion, clear legal standards–are harder to apply. When private companies and data brokers hold detailed profiles on billions of people, state access to that data may expand quietly, without the visibility that once accompanied police or intelligence operations. When AI and predictive tools guide attention, they may entrench biases and obscure responsibility.

The questions raised by these technologies are not purely technical. They are political and ethical. How much surveillance capacity should a state possess, even if it claims to use it benevolently? What constraints and oversight mechanisms are necessary to prevent abuse? How can transparency and accountability be maintained when systems are complex, classified, and operated in partnership with private actors? How should societies respond when foreign and domestic information operations blur the line between persuasion and manipulation?

Technology does not determine the answers. It changes the range of what is possible, both for protection and for control. Secret services can use digital tools to defend against genuine threats or to expand their reach into everyday life. The direction they take depends on law, institutions, political culture, and civic vigilance.

Understanding the digital turn in intelligence is therefore not merely a matter of cataloguing new gadgets and techniques. It is about recognizing how data-driven power alters the relationship between security and freedom–and about insisting that, even in an age of algorithms and global networks, secret services remain subject to principles that protect human dignity and democratic self-government.

In the digital age, secret power increasingly operates through ordinary infrastructures: phones, platforms, cameras, financial systems, location data, and communication networks. Surveillance no longer depends only on hidden rooms or human informants; it often begins with data produced by everyday life and stored by private companies before it becomes useful to the state. Democratic states have always balanced secrecy and accountability, but digital technologies change the scale and the direction of that balance. If intelligence services can monitor whole populations through data trails, if commercial platforms quietly provide detailed behavioral maps, and if these practices are normalised as routine risk management, then the traditional image of a limited state watching defined suspects no longer fits. The danger is not only spectacular abuse, but a slow shift towards a political order in which continuous, invisible monitoring becomes part of how power is routinely exercised. A democracy that accepts this as its new normal does not simply face new security challenges; it silently rewrites its own understanding of what it means to be a free citizen under the rule of law.

Snowden and the Architecture of Mass Surveillance

Edward Snowden's disclosures in 2013 revealed not only specific surveillance programs, but an entire mindset behind them. The documents he provided showed that the U.S. National Security Agency (NSA), often in cooperation with allied services, had built systems for the large-scale collection of communications metadata – records about who communicated with whom, when, and from where – as well as far-reaching access to the content of communications crossing major internet infrastructure and the servers of global technology companies. Programs associated with these revelations, such as PRISM and various forms of upstream collection, demonstrated that what had been presented to the public as targeted surveillance of suspects could in practice involve bulk collection touching millions of ordinary users around the world.

These disclosures made visible a form of "total information awareness" mentality: the belief that, in order to prevent terrorism and other threats, intelligence agencies should aim to collect and retain as much data as technically possible, on the assumption that future analysis might extract relevant patterns. Even when official rhetoric insisted that only metadata were being gathered, not "real" content, Snowden's documents and subsequent debates showed how powerful metadata can be in reconstructing networks, movements, and personal behavior at scale. They also suggested that agencies had worked to circumvent or weaken encryption standards, and had pressed companies for direct or indirect access to data flows, raising broader concerns about the security and integrity of the digital ecosystem as a whole.

This mentality of total information does not only signify a technical leap in capabilities, but also a political reversal in the basic relationship between the state and citizens. Instead of assuming that the individual is left alone until a concrete suspicion arises, the digital infrastructure pushes the system toward the opposite principle: everyone is, by definition, potentially interesting. In such an order, the burden of justifying surveillance no longer falls on institutions, but is, almost imperceptibly, shifted onto citizens, who must live with the assumption that they are already being observed.

The Snowden case also exposed the problem of secret law. Many programs operated under classified interpretations of statutes such as the USA PATRIOT Act and secret decisions of the Foreign Intelligence Surveillance Court. Publicly, citizens saw legal safeguards; privately, key terms had been interpreted in ways that enabled bulk collection.

Snowden's disclosures therefore changed the debate in two ways. First, they replaced abstract suspicions about possible mass surveillance with documentary evidence that such systems existed and were being used on a global scale. Second, they exposed the gap between public law and secret practice: formal rights and safeguards remained on the books, but hidden interpretations had expanded intelligence powers in ways that neither citizens nor many legislators fully understood. The case shows how technical capacity, ambitious collection programs, and secret legal frameworks can push democratic states toward surveillance practices that sit uneasily with their own constitutional principles.

Julian Assange, WikiLeaks, and the Politics of Secrecy

Julian Assange[3] and WikiLeaks occupy a central place in the modern politics of secrecy. Their importance does not lie only in the volume of classified documents they helped bring into public view, but in the way they changed the relationship between states, journalism, technology, war, and public accountability. WikiLeaks showed that in the digital age, secrecy had become both more expansive and more fragile. States could collect, classify, and store information on an unprecedented scale; but the same digital systems that enabled vast secrecy also

3. Julian Assange, the founder of WikiLeaks, became internationally known after WikiLeaks published large collections of U.S. military and diplomatic documents, including materials related to the wars in Iraq and Afghanistan. After years of legal proceedings, he entered a plea agreement with the United States in 2024, pleaded guilty to one charge related to obtaining and disclosing classified national-defense information, was sentenced to time already served, and returned to Australia.

made it possible for large archives to be copied, transmitted, and published across borders.

Assange did not fit easily into the older categories through which democratic societies understood the press. He was not simply a traditional newspaper editor, nor merely a technical activist, nor only a publisher of leaked documents. He stood at the intersection of all these roles. WikiLeaks functioned as a platform for receiving, organizing, and publishing materials that governments and powerful institutions wanted to keep hidden. Its work challenged the assumption that states should retain near-total control over the circulation of classified knowledge, especially when that knowledge concerned war, diplomacy, surveillance, corruption, or abuse of power.

The most consequential WikiLeaks publications were connected to the wars in Iraq and Afghanistan and to United States diplomatic communications. These releases exposed the hidden texture of modern power: military reporting, diplomatic calculation, civilian harm, detention practices, strategic bargaining, and the gap between public language and private assessment. For supporters of WikiLeaks, the publications revealed information that citizens in democratic societies had a right to know. Governments had invoked security, democracy, human rights, and counterterrorism to justify military and diplomatic action; WikiLeaks forced the public to confront what those policies looked like inside the documents of power itself.

This is why the Assange case cannot be reduced to a narrow dispute about leaking classified files. It belongs to a larger struggle over who has the authority to decide what remains secret. States argue that secrecy is necessary to protect sources, operations, diplomacy, and national defense. This argument cannot simply be dismissed; some secrecy is real, and some disclosures can carry risks. But secrecy also protects institutions from embarrassment, shields unlawful or immoral conduct, conceals the human consequences of war, and prevents citizens from judging policies carried out in their name. The democratic problem begins when the language of national security becomes a blanket under which state violence, deception, and impunity can disappear.

Assange became a symbolic figure because he confronted that blanket directly. He treated secrecy not as a sacred privilege of the state, but as a political arrangement that must be tested against public interest. This was the radical core of WikiLeaks: the idea that citizens cannot meaningfully judge power if the most important evidence about power is permanently withheld from them. In that sense, WikiLeaks was not only a publishing project, but an intervention into the architecture of accountability.

The reaction of the state was correspondingly severe. Assange faced years of legal pursuit, confinement, imprisonment, and attempted extradition. To his critics, he had recklessly endangered security and crossed the line from journalism into unlawful acquisition and dissemination of classified material. To his defenders, he was punished because he helped expose the realities of war and challenged the secrecy on which imperial and military power often depend. Both sides used the language of principle, but the asymmetry was unmistakable: on one side stood a publisher and a platform; on the other, the legal, diplomatic, intelligence, and carceral capacities of some of the most powerful states in the world.

The legal case against Assange also raised a profound question for press freedom. If publishing classified information in the public interest can be prosecuted under espionage law, then the boundary between journalism and spying becomes dangerously unstable. Investigative journalism has long depended on leaks, confidential sources, and the publication of information governments would prefer to suppress. Newspapers have published secret documents on wars, surveillance programs, covert operations, and government misconduct. The novelty of WikiLeaks was not that it revealed secrets, but that it did so at digital scale, outside the traditional hierarchy of editorial institutions, and with a confrontational theory of transparency.

That scale made many observers uncomfortable. WikiLeaks did not always operate like a conventional newsroom, and debates about redaction, harm, responsibility, and editorial judgment remain legitimate. But those debates should not obscure the central issue: the prosecution of Assange sent a warning far beyond one person. It suggested that the state might treat the publication of its secrets not as an act to be politically contested, but as an offense to be criminalized. For anyone concerned with intelligence power, this is a decisive point. Secret services and military institutions already operate behind layers of classification. If those who reveal their misconduct face extreme legal consequences, then secrecy becomes not only an operational tool, but a shield against democratic scrutiny.

Assange's eventual plea agreement in 2024 ended his long legal ordeal but did not resolve the underlying conflict. He pleaded guilty to a single charge related to obtaining and disclosing classified U.S. national defense documents and was sentenced to time already served, allowing him to return to Australia. The agreement closed the case procedurally, but it left open the larger political question: should the exposure of state secrets concerning war and public wrongdoing be treated primarily as a crime, or as part of the difficult ecology of democratic accountability? The legal system produced a settlement; it did not produce a moral or political consensus.

For the study of secret services, Assange matters because he reveals the vulnerability of secret power in the digital age. Intelligence agencies and security states depend on classification, compartmentalization, and control over information flows. WikiLeaks showed that those controls can be broken not only by rival states, but by insiders, digital platforms, journalists, activists, and transnational publics. This does not mean that all leaks are justified or that transparency is simple. It means that secrecy is no longer a closed relationship between the state and its own archives. It is now contested across networks, platforms, courts, newsrooms, diplomatic channels, and public opinion.

The Assange case also clarifies the difference between legal accountability and democratic accountability. A state may legally classify information, legally prosecute disclosure, and legally argue that secrecy protects national defense. Yet those legal claims do not automatically settle the democratic question of whether the public had a right to know what was done in its name. Law can protect freedom, but it can also organize silence. In matters of intelligence, war, and empire, the legality of secrecy often coexists with the political necessity of exposure.

Seen in this light, Assange should be understood less as an isolated personality than as a stress test for the modern security state. His case forced liberal democracies to confront a contradiction at their core: they claim legitimacy from informed public consent, yet they often conduct foreign policy, war, surveillance, and intelligence operations through systems of secrecy that make such consent incomplete. WikiLeaks did not eliminate that contradiction, but it made it visible.

The deeper lesson is not that every secret must be published or that every leak is virtuous. The lesson is that secrecy cannot be allowed to define its own limits. Where states possess the power to classify evidence of their own conduct, democratic societies need countervailing forces: investigative journalism, whistleblowers, independent courts, parliamentary scrutiny, civil society, and protected channels for disclosure. Without them, national security becomes a language through which power explains why the public must remain ignorant.

Assange's significance lies precisely there. He exposed not only documents, but a structure: the dependence of modern state power on secrecy, the fragility of public oversight, and the willingness of governments to treat exposure itself as a threat. In a book about secret services, his case belongs not at the margins, but near the center of the digital turn. It shows that the struggle over intelligence power is also a struggle over publication, evidence, memory, and the public's right to see what is done behind the closed doors of security.

Private Firms as Intelligence Actors: Spyware, Data Brokers, and OSINT Companies

The modern intelligence ecosystem is no longer populated only by state agencies. Private companies now sell spyware, harvest and trade personal data, and provide OSINT services to governments, corporations, and other clients. Capabilities once associated mainly with state intelligence services have become commercial products.

For states, these actors are attractive because they provide ready-made tools, access, and analytical capacity without requiring governments to build everything internally. For companies, intelligence-style services promise competitive advantage: corporate security units, risk consultancies, spyware vendors, OSINT firms, and data brokers can identify threats, track activism, map reputational risks, or support cyber reconnaissance. The result is a growing market in which surveillance and intelligence capabilities circulate through contracts, platforms, and informal partnerships.

This blurring of public and private power complicates law and accountability. Private vendors often operate across borders and under weaker transparency rules than state agencies, while their products can help clients bypass traditional surveillance constraints. When a government buys data, tools, or analytical services instead of collecting everything directly, oversight bodies may have difficulty determining where public authority ends and private infrastructure begins.

When Surveillance Is Rented: States, Data Brokers, and Citizens

In many countries, intelligence and security agencies no longer rely only on their own technical systems and legal authorizations to obtain personal data. Instead, they increasingly tap into a commercial ecosystem built by private companies whose core business is collecting, aggregating, and selling information about individuals' movements, habits, and preferences. A particularly revealing example is the market for location data derived from mobile phones and apps.

Commercial data brokers assemble vast datasets that track where people live, work, travel, and spend their time. This information often comes from seemingly innocuous applications: weather apps, fitness trackers, navigation tools, advertising SDKs embedded in other software. Users may click "accept" on lengthy terms of service without fully realizing that their movements will be continuously logged, combined, and sold on to third parties. The result is a detailed map of everyday life: visits to religious institutions, attendance at political meetings, trips to clinics, participation in protests.

Intelligence and law enforcement agencies can obtain access to such datasets by purchasing them from brokers or by using intermediaries who bundle and resell data for "risk analysis," "threat intelligence," or "public safety" purposes. From the agencies' perspective, this approach has two advantages. First, it provides high-resolution information without the need to build and maintain all the necessary collection infrastructure themselves. Second, in some jurisdictions, it allows them to argue that they are not technically "conducting surveillance" in the traditional legal sense, because they are merely buying commercially available information rather than directly intercepting communications or tracking devices.

Formally, the mandate of the services may not change: laws still describe their powers in terms of wiretaps, search warrants, or targeted monitoring. Substantively, however, their reach expands. By renting access to data that companies have already gathered, agencies can reconstruct patterns of movement and association that would once have required individualized court orders, visible operations, or politically sensitive legislation. The legal framework continues to distinguish between "state surveillance" and "commercial profiling," but in practice the two become tightly intertwined.

From a rule-of-law perspective, this raises uncomfortable questions. Oversight bodies and courts may carefully review applications for interception or physical searches while having limited visibility into what types of commercially acquired data agencies use, under what conditions, and with which safeguards. Citizens who might challenge intrusive measures in court are rarely aware that their location history, purchased from a broker, underpins an investigation. Data protection regimes that focus on consumer consent and privacy policies struggle to capture the risks that emerge when commercial and state uses of data converge.

This arrangement exposes how vulnerable citizens become when the intelligence ecosystem overlaps with the infrastructure of the data market. The power of secret services no longer depends solely on their own sensors and warrants; it also rests on the willingness of private actors to monetize personal information and on legal gaps that treat "commercial" and "state" data as fundamentally distinct.

Red Lines in the Digital Security State

Recognising that some surveillance can be compatible with democracy does not mean that every extension of digital power can be justified by invoking security. Liberal constitutionalism depends on hard boundaries that do not move with each new scare or technological possibility.

A first red line is generalized, indiscriminate monitoring of entire populations. Bulk collection and long-term retention of communication or location data from millions of people, without individualized suspicion and strict temporal limits, reverses the basic principle of criminal justice. Instead of intervening when there are reasons, the state quietly assumes that everyone is a potential future suspect.

A second red line is the routine use of intelligence tools against journalism, opposition, and peaceful civil society under the vague banner of extremism or stability. When surveillance is directed not at concrete plots or espionage, but at mapping networks of critics for later leverage, the line between intelligence service and political police has already been crossed, whatever the legal labels say.

A third boundary concerns secret arrangements between states and private corporations that effectively bypass democratic decision-making. Cooperation with platforms, telecom providers, and data brokers may sometimes be necessary, but hidden backdoors, informal data-sharing, and off-the-books purchases of bulk datasets undermine the very idea of public consent.

A fourth red line is the delegation of core decisions about suspicion and risk to opaque automated systems. When individuals are silently scored by algorithms that they cannot see or challenge, and those scores shape whose communications are scrutinised or whose movements are flagged as abnormal, a part of sovereignty migrates from visible institutions into invisible code.

Democratic states will continue to use secret services in the digital age. The question is whether they accept these lines as non-negotiable limits or treat them as flexible obstacles to be worked around when convenient.

Power, Oversight, and the Limits of Reform

Most citizens will never read a classified file, sit in an intelligence briefing, approve a surveillance warrant, or know the name of the analyst whose assessment justified a drone strike, a raid, or the placement of an activist group on a watchlist. Yet the world of secret services can shape their lives profoundly: when states expand surveillance after an attack, when private data becomes material for security assessments, when labor organizing is treated as extremism, or when the boundary between legitimate dissent and criminalized resistance quietly shifts.

This is why intelligence is not only a matter for security professionals. Citizens in democratic societies face a difficult problem: they are asked to trust institutions that operate largely in secret, while history shows that such institutions have sometimes protected state stability, elite interests, and existing economic arrangements more readily than broader forms of collective safety.

The task of critical citizenship is therefore more demanding than simply supporting or rejecting intelligence agencies. It requires recognizing that secret services are not neutral instruments floating above politics. They are institutions shaped by the political, legal, and economic orders in which they operate. Oversight mechanisms can reduce harm, expose abuse, and impose limits, but they cannot by themselves answer the deeper question of what kind of security is being protected, for whom, and at whose expense.

This chapter examines what citizens need to understand about intelligence power, how fear and crisis can expand surveillance, what constraints are possible within existing systems, and why democratic control over secret power requires more than procedural oversight alone.

How Citizens Should Think About Secret Power

Secret services are often described as technical institutions: collectors of information, analysts of threats, protectors of security. Yet their existence and behavior are deeply political. Surveillance powers, covert operations, and definitions of "threat" all reflect choices about whose security matters, which challenges to power are treated as dangerous, and what kinds of resistance are tolerated or suppressed.

For that reason, public thinking about secret services cannot be left only to insiders, security professionals, or procedural reformers. A critical understanding requires citizens who can ask uncomfortable questions: Whose security do these institutions protect? What social order do they help preserve? And can agencies shaped by the defense of state and economic order be redirected toward genuinely democratic forms of security?

What Citizens Need to Understand

Citizens do not need expert knowledge of classified operations or technical systems. But several insights are essential for informed engagement with intelligence power.

First, secret services should not be understood as protecting "society" in the abstract. In many historical contexts, they have protected the interests of states, governing elites, dominant institutions, and powerful economic actors. While intelligence agencies formally claim to defend "national security" and "public safety," the historical record shows that those concepts can be interpreted in ways that privilege state stability, property relations, geopolitical influence, and elite political order.

This does not mean every intelligence action is reducible to class interest or corporate power. It means that intelligence institutions often operate within systems where some interests are more readily recognized as "security" than others. Labor militancy, anti-colonial struggles, anti-war activism, socialist organizing, environmental resistance, and racial justice movements have all, in different contexts, been treated as threats not because they were always violent, but because they challenged existing arrangements of power.

These patterns are difficult to explain solely as isolated abuses or "mission creep." They suggest deeper institutional tendencies that deserve scrutiny. COINTELPRO, for example, was not merely an isolated departure from normal practice; it revealed how intelligence institutions can interpret radical political movements as threats to state order.

Second, the concept of "threat" is never purely neutral. What counts as terrorism rather than resistance, extremism rather than legitimate organizing, or subversion rather than political speech often depends on who has the authority to define danger. Environmental activists, labor organizers, anti-war movements, racial justice campaigns, and anti-capitalist groups may be viewed through a security lens when their actions disrupt powerful interests. At the same time, corporate wrongdoing, union-busting, environmental destruction, or state violence may be framed as legal, economic, or administrative matters rather than security threats.

This reveals an important asymmetry: security language often translates social conflict into a problem of order. Citizens should therefore ask not only whether a threat exists, but who defines it, who benefits from that definition, and which forms of harm remain invisible.

Third, oversight mechanisms in democratic societies face structural limits. Parliamentary committees, judicial review, and independent watchdogs can reduce abuses and create space for accountability. But they usually operate within the same legal and political frameworks that define what counts as a legitimate security concern. They may examine whether procedures were followed without always questioning whether the underlying category of "threat" was politically distorted.

This does not make oversight meaningless. It can constrain abuse, delay dangerous operations, expose unlawful practices, and provide tools for civil society and courts. But oversight alone cannot resolve deeper conflicts over whose safety matters, which interests are protected, and how far intelligence agencies should be allowed to treat political disruption as a security problem.

Fourth, secrecy is both a practical necessity and a democratic danger. Some secrecy may be justified to protect sources, methods, and ongoing operations. But permanent secrecy can also insulate power from accountability. When citizens cannot know who is surveilled, on what basis, with what evidence, and subject to what review, democratic consent becomes fragile.

With these understandings, citizens can approach debates about intelligence power not only as a question of "balancing security and freedom," but by asking: security for whom, at whose expense, and in defense of what kind of social order?

Fear, Crisis, and the Expansion of Surveillance

Public support for expanded intelligence powers often rises after crises: terrorist attacks, geopolitical shocks, economic instability, or social upheaval. Fear is not always manufactured; many threats are real. But crisis can also create conditions in which extraordinary powers are introduced quickly, debated poorly, and normalized over time.

A familiar pattern appears across many democratic systems:

A crisis occurs or is framed as imminent.

Security officials argue that existing powers are insufficient.

New measures are introduced under time pressure.

Temporary powers become permanent.

The definition of "threat" gradually expands beyond the original emergency.

To distinguish genuine security needs from political manipulation, citizens can ask several questions.

Who defines the threat, and whose interests does that definition serve?

After 9/11, the language of counterterrorism justified real efforts to prevent attacks, but it also enabled wars, mass surveillance, and the monitoring of Muslim communities and anti-war movements.

What evidence supports the claim that new powers are necessary?

Failures are often attributed to insufficient surveillance, even when the deeper problem was poor analysis, ignored warnings, political pressure, or bad coordination between agencies.

Who will be targeted in practice, regardless of formal mandates?

Laws framed as targeting terrorists, extremists, or foreign agents can be extended to activists, labor organizers, racial justice movements, environmental groups, or left-wing organizations.

Do the proposed powers include sunset clauses, independent review, and mechanisms for reversal?

Emergency powers often outlive the emergencies that justified them.

What alternatives have been excluded from debate?

If the only policy question is "how much surveillance is needed," then broader questions about war, inequality, policing, poverty, racism, and foreign policy disappear from view.

Fear can be a rational response to real danger. But policy made under intense fear often gives lasting power to security institutions, while the promised safety remains uncertain.

What Constraints Are Possible Within Existing Systems?

Recognizing the political role of intelligence agencies does not mean reform is impossible or worthless. Legal constraints, public oversight, and institutional checks can reduce immediate harm, protect vulnerable communities, and create space for democratic challenge. The question is what can realistically be achieved within existing systems, and what limits those achievements carry.

Minimal Standards for Legitimate Surveillance

Even within existing systems, democratic societies can insist on constraints that limit the worst abuses.

1. Narrow, legally defined mandates

Surveillance powers should be restricted to serious threats such as imminent violence, espionage, sabotage, or attacks on critical infrastructure. Vague categories such as "public order" or "extremism" invite political policing.

2. Individualized authorization by independent judges

The most intrusive measures – intercepting private communications, planting malware, entering homes, or long-term monitoring – should require warrants based on specific evidence against identifiable targets. Bulk collection and dragnet surveillance weaken the presumption of innocence.

3. Mandatory logging and ex-post review

Every surveillance action should leave an auditable trail accessible to oversight bodies and, after appropriate time and redaction, to the public. Invisible surveillance makes accountability nearly impossible.

4. Functional parliamentary and independent oversight

Legislative committees, independent commissioners, inspectors general, and specialized courts can impose discipline on intelligence agencies if they have real access, legal authority, technical expertise, and political will.

5. Whistleblower protections and public reporting

Officials who expose illegal activity, political targeting, or systemic abuse need credible legal protections. Public reporting on surveillance powers, warrant numbers, categories of targets, and oversight findings should be as detailed as security permits.

These constraints matter. They can prevent some abuses, expose others, and provide legal tools for resistance. But they face inherent limits.

The Structural Limits of Oversight

Even robust oversight mechanisms operate within systems that define some interests as legitimate and others as threatening. Several recurring weaknesses follow from this.

Class and institutional bias

Parliamentarians approving budgets, judges issuing warrants, and commissioners reviewing programs often come from political, legal, and administrative elites. This does not mean they are dishonest, but it does mean they may share assumptions about property, order, stability, and reasonable uses of state power.

Secrecy as shield

Oversight bodies themselves often operate in secrecy. Citizens may not know what questions were asked, what information was withheld, what abuses were ignored, or what compromises were accepted. This can create a gap between formal oversight and democratic accountability.

Threat inflation and selective disclosure

Agencies often control much of the information that reaches overseers. By emphasizing certain dangers and withholding other contexts, they can shape the frame through which oversight bodies interpret events.

Revolving doors and cultural capture

Former intelligence officials may advise oversight bodies; oversight staff may later move into security or private intelligence careers. Such relationships can create expertise, but also shared assumptions and reluctance to confront agencies too directly.

The fundamental problem is that oversight often assumes a shared understanding of "proper" intelligence work. But when political movements are defined as threats to order, what reformers describe as abuse may sometimes reflect broader features of the system rather than isolated misconduct.

What Democratic Societies Must Refuse

If some constraints are possible within existing systems, certain practices should be treated as incompatible with even minimal democratic standards. Drawing red lines matters because it clarifies what a society should not normalize.

Red Line 1: Mass, suspicionless surveillance of entire populations

Collecting metadata on everyone, storing communications in bulk, recording web activity, or tracking physical movement "just in case" inverts the logic of justice. It treats citizens as potential suspects and creates an infrastructure that can later be used against political opposition or social movements.

Red Line 2: Systematic targeting of political expression, journalism, and social movements

When intelligence tools are routinely used to map journalists' sources, infiltrate protest movements, compile dossiers on activists, or disrupt lawful organizing, the line between intelligence and political policing has been crossed.

Red Line 3: Secret partnerships with corporations that bypass democratic process

When states purchase bulk data from brokers, pressure platforms into hidden cooperation, or rely on private surveillance infrastructures, legal limits on state power can be quietly bypassed.

Red Line 4: Algorithmic classification systems without transparency or appeal

Automated risk-scoring that places individuals on watchlists, restricts travel, triggers investigations, or justifies pre-emptive intervention can create new forms of opaque control. Any system that exercises power over citizens must allow explanation, challenge, and correction.

Versions of these red lines are already being tested or weakened in many democracies. Naming them matters because it clarifies what is at stake.

Beyond Reform: What Fundamental Change Would Require

Reforms, oversight, and legal constraints can reduce harm within existing systems. But they may not fully resolve a deeper contradiction: institutions built to protect existing state and economic orders are difficult to transform into instruments of genuinely collective security.

A more democratic understanding of security would require several shifts.

First, the definition of security must be widened. Security should not mean only protection of state stability, property rights, borders, and elite continuity. It should also include protection from poverty, exploitation, state violence, workplace harm, environmental destruction, and war.

Second, surveillance capitalism must be confronted. As long as private corporations profit from large-scale data collection and states can access that data for intelligence purposes, surveillance will continue to expand beyond traditional legal categories. Regulating intelligence agencies is not enough if the data infrastructure they rely on is built by private actors.

Third, institutions of secrecy must be subjected to stronger democratic control. A society committed to public freedom cannot allow permanent secrecy to become a normal condition of government. Some secrecy may remain necessary, but it must be narrow, justified, reviewed, and contestable.

Fourth, reform requires public pressure. Major constraints on intelligence power have rarely emerged from elite benevolence alone. They have usually followed scandals, journalism, whistleblowing, court challenges, civil society campaigns, and social movements that made secrecy politically costly.

These transformations are difficult, but they show why the debate cannot stop at technical oversight. The deeper question is how societies define security and who has the power to contest that definition.

The Responsibility of Critical Citizenship

For citizens navigating intelligence power in democratic societies, the task is dual.

Tactically, they should demand stronger constraints within existing systems: support whistleblowers, defend civil liberties organizations, challenge expansive surveillance laws, expose political targeting, and use legal tools to resist abuse. These struggles matter because they protect vulnerable communities and create space for public accountability.

Strategically, citizens should recognize that procedural reforms cannot solve every structural problem. Intelligence agencies are likely to reflect the priorities of the societies and states that create them. Meaningful security therefore requires not only better oversight, but broader democratic struggle over inequality, state power, corporate influence, policing, war, and public control.

This means rejecting both liberal complacency and conspiratorial despair. Oversight alone will not solve everything; but it is also false that nothing can be done. The struggle over secret power is ongoing, contested, and partial – but it is real.

How Citizens Respond: Lessons from Post-Scandal Surveillance Debates

In several democracies, surveillance scandals have shown that citizens are not merely passive objects of secret power. After the Snowden disclosures in 2013, protests, online campaigns, civil-society coalitions, NGOs, journalists, and experts helped translate complex surveillance programs into public debate and pressure for reform.

In the years that followed, courts in the United States and Europe ruled against parts of bulk collection and data-retention regimes, while legislatures adopted laws that tightened surveillance requirements, increased transparency, or created additional oversight mechanisms. These reforms were incomplete and contested, but they showed that public pressure can reshape the limits of intelligence authorities.

Secrecy, Power, and the Horizon of Freedom

Secret services are not the hidden masters of history, but they are institutions through which states and governing elites have often managed challenges to their authority. Understanding them requires moving beyond myths of neutral expertise and asking how secrecy, surveillance, and covert power can defend existing political, economic, and social orders.

A free society cannot abolish secrecy entirely under current conditions. But it can refuse the normalization of permanent, invisible scrutiny as the background of everyday life. It can resist the framing of dissent as extremism, organizing as subversion, and resistance as terrorism. It can demand that oversight mechanisms function with transparency, independence, and real power. And it can build public movements capable of forcing deeper reforms.

The central question is not only under what conditions secret services can protect freedom, but whose freedom they protect, from what threats, and for what purpose. Until those questions are answered in democratic and genuinely collective terms, intelligence power will remain vulnerable to becoming not only an instrument of security, but also an instrument of domination.

The final responsibility belongs not only to agencies, governments, or oversight bodies, but to citizens who refuse both naive trust and fatalistic acceptance. The struggle over secret power is therefore inseparable from broader struggles over democracy, social power, and public control – and those struggles are far from over.

Schneier, Bruce. *Data and Goliath: The Hidden Battles to Collect Your Data and Control Your World.*

Security Intelligence Review Committee, Canada. *Annual Reports on the Oversight of Intelligence Services.*

Shue, Henry. "Torture in Dreamland: Disposing of the Ticking Bomb."

Soldatov, Andrei, and Irina Borogan. *The New Nobility: The Restoration of Russia's Security State and the Enduring Legacy of the KGB.*

Solove, Daniel J. *Understanding Privacy.*

Stan, Lavinia, ed. *Transitional Justice in Post-Communist Romania: The Politics of Memory.*

Stiglitz, Joseph E. *Globalization and Its Discontents.*

Stoycheff, Elizabeth. "Under Surveillance: Examining Facebook's Spiral of Silence Effects in the Wake of NSA Internet Monitoring."

The Guardian. "The Snowden Files." Series of articles on PRISM, TEMPORA, and other NSA/GCHQ operations.

Thomas, Gordon. *Gideon's Spies: The Secret History of the Mossad.*

Thomas, Nigel. *Yugoslav Armies 1941–2001.*

UK Intelligence and Security Committee. *Privacy and Security: A Modern and Transparent Legal Framework.*

U.S. Senate Select Committee on Intelligence. *Report on the U.S. Intelligence Community's Prewar Intelligence Assessments on Iraq.*

U.S. Senate Select Committee on Intelligence. *Committee Study of the CIA's Detention and Interrogation Program.*

Wallace, Robert, and H. Keith Melton. *Spycraft: The Secret History of the CIA's Spytechs, from Communism to Al-Qaeda.*

Wala, Michael. *Der Bundesnachrichtendienst: Von den Anfängen bis 1968.*

Weiner, Tim. *Legacy of Ashes: The History of the CIA.*

Zuboff, Shoshana. *The Age of Surveillance Capitalism: The Fight for a Human Future at the New Frontier of Power.*

www.ingramcontent.com/pod-product-compliance
Ingram Content Group UK Ltd.
Pitfield, Milton Keynes, MK11 3LW, UK
UKHW021341020826
14184UKWH00028B/621

9 798196 288869